ROSEMARY FRIEDMAN has published twenty-six books (fiction, non-fiction and memoir) which have been widely translated and serialized on radio, as well as more than fifty short stories syndicated worldwide. Her three stage plays were produced in London and Poland and have toured the UK. She is a voting member of BAFTA and has served on the executive committees of the Society of Authors and PEN where she worked on behalf of Writers in Prison. She has four daughters and ten grandchildren and lives in London.

Also By Rosemary Friedman

FINAL DRAFT

Reflections on Life

ROSEMARY FRIEDMAN

*For Daniel —
with love —
Rosemary Friedman
14/09/17*

PETER OWEN

London and Chicago

PETER OWEN PUBLISHERS

Conway Hall, 25 Red Lion Square, London WC1R 4RL

Peter Owen books are distributed in the USA and Canada by
Independent Publishers Group/Trafalgar Square
814 North Franklin Street, Chicago, IL 60610

First published in Great Britain 2017 by Peter Owen Publishers

ISBN 978-0-7206-1961-4

A catalogue record for this book is available from the British Library.

Printed and bound by Printworks Global Limited, London/Hong Kong.

'Peace and War' ('Mein Offizier') first published in *Besiegt, Befreit* . . .
C. Bertelsmann, Munich, 1995
'My Grandmother's Chicken Soup' first published in the *Jewish Quarterly*, 2014
'On Growing Old' longlisted for the William Hazlitt Essay Prize, 2015

Thanks are due to Antonia Owen, Nick Kent, Nadia Manuelli, Luisa Conde, Barnaby Spiro, Guy Shapir, Amelia Richards, Miranda Spiro, Murdoch Rawson and all at Peter Owen Ltd. for their input and assistance with *Final Draft*.

In loving memory of Dennis Friedman,
husband, friend, companion, champion,
mentor, confidant, physician, guru –
and editor par excellence

CONTENTS

PREFACE

An essay (or reflection), according to Aldous Huxley, is 'a literary device for saying almost everything about anything'. As definitions go, Huxley's is no more or less accurate than Francis Bacon's 'dispersed meditations' or Samuel Johnson's 'loose sally of the mind'. The originator of the form, however, was the French nobleman, Michel de Montaigne, a sixteenth-century social philosopher. Since he adopted the term 'essay' to describe his attempts at self-portrayal, the particular style of writing has resisted any universal definition. In its broadest sense, the term essay (from the French '*essayer*' to try) may refer to just about any brief piece of non-fiction: an editorial, a critical study, even an excerpt from a book. A more literary definition draws distinctions between an article, read primarily for content, and an essay or reflection, in which the pleasure of reading takes precedence over the information in the text. According to Samuel Johnson, the essay was 'an irregular, undigested piece', and while it can be informal, personal, intimate or relaxed it can, at the same time, be dogmatic and impersonal. What a gift to the writer who can adopt any persona – according to mood or subject matter – and comment on daily life through his or her recollections. Whereas a short story aims to make us 'think', a reflection makes us 'feel', conveying a sense of human presence that is related to the author's deepest sense of self. A basic aspect of the relationship between the writer and the reader is that what the writer says is literally true. The implied contract is about the kind of truth being offered and the writer's ability to convince the reader that his or her knowledge of the world is valid. The author invites him or her to accept as authentic a certain kind of experience as he or she conveys moods, fantasies, whims, chance reflections and random observations.

Montaigne used his essays to inform the reader of everything that came into his head, sharing his experience of what it was like to be human. His exploration of his own life was unlike anything previously written, as he began watching, questioning and writing down all that he observed: 107 free-floating pieces with such diverse titles as 'Of Friendship', 'Of Cannibals', 'How We Laugh and Cry at the Same Thing', 'Of Smells and Odours', none of which attempt to explain or to teach anything. Four hundred years later, readers still come to him in search of wisdom and entertainment. Montaigne held that 'each man is a good education to himself, provided he has the capacity to spy on himself from close up'.

While learning the best strategy to adopt if you are 'held up by armed robbers' may seem arcane in the twenty-first century, advice on 'how to deal with a bully' or 'what do you say to your dog when he wants to go out and play while you want to stay at your desk and get on with your book' are still relevant. Rather than postulating answers to these conundrums, Montaigne leaves us to decide on courses of action for ourselves. He was less interested in what people ought to do than in what they actually did. Much of what he asked himself was pragmatic and is as pertinent today as it was 400 years ago. Preoccupations such as 'how to cope with the fear of death' or the 'loss of a child', how to 'avoid getting into a point-less argument with your wife', 'how to make the most of every moment' or 'in which position to have sex', are timeless and universal. Had Montaigne lived today he would perhaps have veered towards psychiatry or at the very least delved into the benefits of Cognitive Behaviour Therapy. *Plus ça change, plus c'est la même chose.* From Shakespeare to Pinter a human being is a human being, and while the world may have changed the psyche has not aged. Montaigne simply wrote down what was going through his head when he picked up his pen, capturing states of mind as they happened. Using himself as a template, he delved into every aspect of life and, like any psychotherapist, was curious about what drove people to do what they did. With no regard for rationality he allowed his thoughts to meander and was unconcerned if they wandered off – which they were inclined to do – in contradictory and unpredictable directions. 'It is the only book in the world of its kind,' he wrote, 'a book with a wild and eccentric plan.' It was not written in neat order from beginning to end but grew, by slow encrustation, like a coral reef.

While this centuries-long conversation is about Michel de Montaigne, a true Renaissance man, it is also about ourselves and holds the proverbial mirror up to nature. In essays or reflec-tions, as in life, there are no easy answers, no neat solutions.

The old Yiddish saying postulates that 'it is easy to sit on the fire with someone else's *tuchos*'. Montaigne is brave enough to put his own backside into the flames and tell us what it feels like. While he often posits conflicting conclusions, reading his dissertations reassures us that there are more ways than one to conduct our lives and many ways to live. If he contradicts himself – putting one thing on one page and the opposite on the next – then, like the poet Walt Whitman – he contradicts himself. One only comes to the truth by learning to do so.

In the following chapters I have attempted to hold the proverbial mirror up to nature, to go with the flow and not to worry if my conclusions are at odds. If they ignite some spark in the reader, this, my 'final draft', will, in the words of the vernacular, have hit the intended spot.

Rosemary Friedman

1

GROWING OLD

Inside every old person is a young person
wondering what happened.

– Terry Pratchett

How *does* it happen? We, who once climbed professional ladders, ran marathons, won medals and prizes now find ourselves queuing for attention at the GP's surgery or in out-patient clinics. Even as we sit there we know that the now unfamiliar body is not a true reflection of ourselves and that given the right prescriptions, the correct potions, we shall throw away our walking aids and soon be better.

It used to be *them*, skirting the hazards and avoiding the uneven paving stones, impeding our progress. Now it is *us*. Having managed to get out of bed you make it to the bathroom where you take a Spartan shower (courtesy of Age UK) which does nothing for the dreams you once had, the plans you once made in the sybaritic tub. Once you are in your eighties (if you are one of the unlucky ones) you enter another world where doing the simplest of tasks is no longer simple.

Dressing takes for ever, stretching and stooping, struggling to access your feet when it comes to the socks. That done there is the kitchen to tackle. The kettle is heavy. You take care, as everyone – despite your protests that you may be old but you are not a halfwit – has drummed in to you. There are cautionary voices in your ears as you reach for the coffee. But what is this? The jar is a new one. You cannot open it. Somewhere there is a gadget. You can't remember where you put it. You reach for a teabag. The microwave is a godsend; porridge in two minutes. Lately you have opted for ready-meals, with their hideous lists of hideous ingredients, where once you were a talented and enthusiastic cook.

'If you're not having a good old age, the fault isn't in old age but in you.' Cicero got it wrong. What's good about an old age in which you are visited if not by Cicero's dreaded 'Crab', by lapses of memory – senior moments! – creaking knees, impaired vision, diminished hearing, irregular heartbeat, a tendency to misplace your misshapen feet which are no longer up to the job. That pathetic female struggling to retrieve coins from her purse at the supermarket checkout cannot be you; that 'tattered coat upon a stick', as Yeats expressed it, is surely not the high-flyer, the public figure who once held sway over empires. Where did it all go wrong?

Disillusioned by the world about us and convinced that our civilization is going the way of Ancient Rome, we struggle to accommodate the intricacies of 'tweet' and 'twitter', attempt to take on board the language of virtual reality. Do we really want a thousand strangers to 'follow' us? What comfort is 'Facebook' when the chips are down?

While for Cicero ageing was 'a heavier load to bear than Mount Etna', Michelangelo did some of his finest work long after middle age, Isaac Newton made an important discovery for every one of his eighty-five years, and Claude Monet, despite his failing eyesight, gave us his *Water Lilies* well into his ninth decade. But what happens if you were once a skilled craftsman or a keen sportsman and must now strive merely to prolong life in the hope that Death may find you planting your cabbages?

What you failed to do when you were young you cannot make up for when you have subsided into serenity of thought and behaviour. We oldies have time enough on our hands but have not only been robbed of the tools with which to finish the job but have been driven to early graves by well-meaning busybodies who prematurely confiscate the cars of the safest road users in the country – condemning them to sit at home dribbling – while their licences are still clean. How unfair is that?

We live in an ageist society where older people are assumed to be incapable long before they are, but as much as we may welcome the maturity of old age – not a privilege granted to everyone – we soon become fragile not only of head but of heart. The merest slight, real or imagined, can wound us, especially if we have 'lost' a cherished companion and no longer have anyone with whom to sit in amicable silence or share the nuts and bolts of the day.

So please do not patronize us because we are on the waiting list for hip replacements or have become defined by our Freedom Passes. A 'non-person' is still a person and, while time is no longer an ally, we have, perhaps, more uses than you think. Under cover of our disabilities, unconstrained by appearances or worried how we seem to others, we are free to observe a world which has metamorphosed since 'our day', without fear of detection. Perhaps it is time for closer examination of these 'non-people' as they reluctantly downsize, relinquish family homes, give away or sell their *lares* and *penates* as they head towards the ignominy of the care home whether state-funded or – for those who lucky enough to be able to afford it – up-market with their own baristas and accommodation for pets.

While the 'second half of life' catches some people by surprise, we have lived the life, we have loved and been loved, we have read the books, we have danced the dance and we still have something to offer. Talk to us. Those of you who are hard-wired to define people by the date on their birth certificates or by their physical appearance, may – reminded for a brief moment of your own mortality – offer us a seat on the bus, but how often do you engage us in conversation? To grow old is not to grow obsolete, to become puppets, devoid of feeling. Ageing, which often brings with it wisdom, represents a new stage of life rather than a slow march towards the end of it. Today's 'senior citizens' have lived through the most tumultuous period in human history, yet at best you ignore us, infantilize us, pity rather than respect us. The outcome of the Second World War – our war – during which we grew up was by no stretch of the imagination a *fait accompli*. Many of us lost loved ones, risked lives, were shunted round the country with labels round our necks, existed on meagre rations, were bombed out of our homes, spent days in air-raid shelters or stumbled around like zombies through blacked-out streets. Mercifully, unlike the images you capture so easily on your mobile devices (where they remain *ad infinitum* unprinted), we still have a record of these drama-filled times in our fading photograph albums in which, at some later date, you just might be interested. Take heed and have a little patience, a little more respect for those who know full well that the race of men is like the race of leaves and that, sooner or later, those leaves must fall. Do not airbrush us prematurely out of your lives.

Conscious of our physical condition, those of us who can no longer get around do our crosswords, play Scrabble, listen to the radio, watch the goggle-box or sit by the window waiting for 'meals on wheels'. Others with more robust social connections, for whom 'the utility of living consists not in the length of days but in the use of time', as Montaigne put it, join choirs or book clubs or follow courses at the University of the Third Age in a final quest for knowledge. Whatever our preferences or capabilities we cannot hold back the advancing years. Perhaps 'growing well' into old age is not about striving to be young but about accepting life in all its complexities, accepting it with strength, accepting loss and disability as well as opportunities for new experiences and developing a balance of hope over despair. What lies behind you and what lies in front of you pales in comparison to what lies inside you.

While acknowledging that life ceases for us just as we are getting ready for it, that we've 'had a good innings' and that 'it's time to hang up our bats', perhaps we should learn to appreciate the fact that the inner, psychic time is different from the outer, chronological time, that it is not about the amount of money, the honours or the wisdom that have accrued but about the attitude of mind and the realization that the afternoon of life can be as meaningful as the morning. 'Growing old' is a bore, but it is the only way to live a long time. Given the health and strength, perhaps we should look it firmly in the eye and, in the words of the vernacular, 'Get over it.'

2

CAN A TEXT
REPLACE A HUG?

Modern technology can't replace
a real-life hug.

– *The Times* leader, 9 June 2017

The twenty-first century seems to be populated by people not only constantly checking, scrolling, clicking and watching but fascinated by their own personae. Permanently attached to their mobile phones, they vie with one another for attention, communicate through sites such as Facebook, Twitter, Instagram, LinkedIn and Tumblr, explore their fantasies ('sexting') in a perpetual celebration of the self and take mind-numbing pictures of anything that moves.

We are all addicted, and our obsession with the internet – 50 per cent of users spend between two and four hours staring at their smartphones every day – is beginning to affect our health, and being constantly connected in this way paradoxically *disconnects* us from each other, reducing our ability to form meaningful relationships. The more time a person spends online, the less time remains for real-life contact, and by stripping away verbal nuance and facial expression and discouraging directness clear communication becomes increasingly difficult.

Preferring texts to conversation, and often dealing with hundreds of messages a day, most teenagers have never physically 'visited' any of the many thousands of 'friends' with whom they are 'in touch', although they feel that they have an intimate knowledge of them via the umbilical cords of their devices through which they get regular 'hits' of pleasure. According to psychologists, social media websites, designed to help people 'connect', are merely causing them to feel increasingly isolated. Binge-watching films and TV box sets on screen, listening to endless podcasts and video-streaming services increase the segregation. On a more worrying note, thousands of children have been investigated by police for sending sexual imagery online and on their phones, and children as young as seven have been involved in what, according to the police, is a 'sexting epidemic'.

It is now more than quarter of a century since, almost without fanfare, the worldwide web, a massive, unregulated experiment on mankind, went live and the secrets of human existence were silently transferred to the 'brains' of machines. The web is now estimated to be used by 3.5 billion people (including 25 per cent of the over-65s) and is one of the greatest innovations of our time. For those of us who are even marginally media-savvy it is hard to imagine life without it. Since its launch, and subsequent evolution, it has not only changed the way we interact with each other but provides us with 24/7 access to world news, travel, entertainment, weather, medicine (diagnoses and treatment) and a virtual world of information. If you went back in time and told the man in the street that ten years on we would be lying in our beds, standing at the bus stop or walking to school or work with eyes permanently glued to a small rectangular apparatus – a portable dopamine pump – on which our very lives depended, he would look at you askance. That is what we do. Like the electric light bulb, this ubiquitous contrivance, this *sine qua non*, this portable game-changer, has transformed the way we eat, sleep, work, live, reproduce, carry out almost every other human activity to the point of laying ourselves open to some form of behavioural obsession to which children – babies who play with iPads before they can walk and toddlers obsessed with screens – do not get off scot-free. Digital technology is advancing at such speed that computers could soon solve every existing problem and, according to the experts, will one day be able to communicate with us as if they were human, anticipating our behaviour and our priorities.

Facebook is the free entry-level social-networking platform that allows users to create profiles, upload photographs and videos, send messages, promote businesses and keep in touch with friends and family. This was something that those over twenty-five used to do by means of the written word, the telephone and face-to-face conversation. According to statistics, internet users now spend more time 'texting' (sending messages) than on any other form of communication. It employs algorithms (codes that tell a computer what to do) to predict our preferences.

Twitter, the social-media, news and micro-blogging service has 3 million users who are said to spend one minute a day 'tweeting', while for the 319 million devotees of Facebook the average use is fifty minutes, with the under-sixteens spending up to *three* hours a day – when they could be doing their homework. Twitter allows anyone with something to say to communicate with 'followers' and to indicate, through a 'heart' emoticon, whether they approve of a message. Dismissed by Luddites as 'a conduit for people who have nothing going on between their ears, or nothing going on in their lives', these 'posts' – snappy notes of 140 characters or less – are referred to as 'tweets', possibly because they are imagined to mimic the short, sweet chirps of Twitter's little bluebird logo. Those who use Twitter to disseminate their views to as many followers as possible are known as 'posters', while those who trawl for and interact with the opinions of others are 'readers'. When someone disagrees vehemently (and sometimes aggressively) with what has been posted they are categorized as 'trolls'.

The internet is a means of connecting a computer to another computer anywhere in the world via dedicated routers and servers, through which all kinds of information, including text, graphics, voice, video and computer programs, can be sent. The fibre-optic cables through which the bulk of the data travels are owned by the telecommunications companies in their respective countries.

While Facebook and Twitter are about words, Instagram is about 'pictures'. Go to any park or open space and you will find visitors of all ages and ethnicity snapping themselves – by means of a 'selfie' (a self-portrait taken on a mobile phone, often on the end of a 'selfie stick') – as well as clicking on images of importunate squirrels and piles of fallen leaves, which misguided photographers imagine will be of fascination to the folks back home. By the same token, in a display of 'one-upmanship' they may also have captured a likeness of the eggs, mushrooms, tomatoes, sausages, bacon and black pudding, which they had on their hotel plates for breakfast.

Snapchat, which in many cases has superceded Instagram, is an ephemeral messaging service by which photographs and videos will (conveniently) self-destruct after ten seconds, the point being that you don't leave a digital footprint and can share pornographic or zany pictures of yourself – doing naked press-ups or brushing your teeth – without feeling self-conscious.

Most of us know what 'emojis' are: smiley or downcast icons we attach to messages to indicate a mood. How many people are aware, however, that, as the dating culture goes viral, the 'aubergine' emoji means not the shiny purple vegetable but an invitation to have sex? By the same token 'Netflix and chill' refers not to the opportunity to curl up on the sofa in front of the TV but to head for the bedroom for a one-night stand.

LinkedIn is a site designed specifically for the business community. It allows registered members to establish and document networks of people they know and trust professionally.

Those readers who are still with me, no matter in which far outpost they live, must have come across the twentieth-century neologism 'Google', the brand name of a leading inter-net search engine, founded in 1998, that has changed the way we process data found on the 'information highway'. The term 'google' (a creative spelling of *googol*, a number equal to 10 to the 100th power), was coined in the 1930s and attributed to the nine-year-old nephew of American mathematician Edward Kasner. Both a noun and a verb (to google), Google searches the worldwide web for information, making the cumbersome volumes of the *Encyclopaedia Britannica* redundant. Without leaving your chair you can inform yourself of just about anything, from the whereabouts of sustainable fishing to the history of the French Revolution. Like it or not, we live in a 'googlecentric' world.

Wikipedia, founded in January 2001, is a free open-content *vade mecum* created through the collaborative efforts of a community of users known as the 'Wikipedians'. While anyone can register to write articles for publication, no registration is needed to edit them.

From the business perspective, social media makes it easy for customers to inform anyone who is interested whether their experiences with a particular internet company are good or bad. This allows advertisers to respond very quickly to both positive and negative feedback, to attend to consumers' problems and maintain, regain or rebuild confidence.

Some of the most sought-after uses of the internet are the online dating sites with their tantalizing promises for the girls (and boys) of finding Prince Charming and for the boys (and girls) of finding their fairytale princesses with whom they can enjoy a brief conversation, a one-night stand or – in the ideal scenario – to live happily ever after. This 'pig in a poke', or 'lucky-dip' method of finding Mr or Mrs Right, is anything but new.

Tinder, launched on the web four years ago, is – like Grindr – a social catalyst that can, and does, change lives. It is a location-based mobile dating agency which means that a generation of men and women, mainly aged under forty-five, need never know what it feels like to be rejected. The use of a simple screen 'swipe', right (accept) or left (reject) the offer of an assignation with the applicant, has revolutionized what was hitherto known as dating. The stigma of online relationships has been slowly lifting, and Tinder facilitates 1.3 million assignations a week, with 9.6 million daily users. Tinder marriages (120,000 a year), as well as casual 'hook-ups', are now the norm.

As early as 1700, barely a decade after the invention of the newspaper as we know it, the first matrimonial services – small ads on behalf of single men and women desperate to find a husband or wife – were created. By the time it came to the Victorian era there was an epidemic of loneliness in 'the city of dreadful solitude' that was London. The working classes, many of whom lived in solitary 'digs' or bed-sits, would join the 'Monkey Rank' (in which they dressed up in their Sunday best and eyed each other while parading up and down on opposite sides of the street) to meet their sweethearts. At the other end of the social spectrum, the aristocracy relied on 'the Season', in which relationships were forged at sporting events, musical evenings or balls.

In the absence of social media, the romantic aspirations of the 'middle classes' were catered for by the Wedding Ring Circle which issued a monthly publication called *The Roundabout* (precursor of today's tabloids) in which the esoteric appellation 'A 100' would indicate to the cognoscenti that the advertiser was male and 'B122' that she was female. Early twentieth-century hotspots for romantic encounters were the Palm Court dances held on the marble floors of up-market hotels such as the Waldorf Astoria in London.

Kiss.com and Match.com (1994 and 1995) were the first online internet services to match people based on 'likes' and 'dislikes', while today's more sophisticated sites – such as www.veggiedate.org – cater for specific groups and require commitment to certain lifestyles. The stigma of online dating has slowly disappeared, and today more than 20 million people a month visit at least one site such as Facebook, Myspace, EliteSingles or Harmony. The result of this, according to *Online Dating Magazine*, is that 120,000 'internet marriages' take place every year.

Where does this leave the bemused minority who may just about have come to terms with the smartphone (with oversized keys for the old folk) but who are bamboozled by the desktop, the laptop and the tablet, the multifarious secrets of which they are too old or too confused to fathom. A study has shown that children check their smartphones on average more than 200 times a day. As parents watch them, their offsprings' thumbs at the ready, communicating with each other from their beds, on the bus or underground, or – in a display of execrable manners beneath the dinner table (if they happen to be eating at one) – and wonder what exactly they are doing, they face the unpalatable truth that, as far as the alternative online world is concerned, they are out of the loop.

While the first generation to come of age on social media – which has been blamed for a surge in teenage depression – open Spotify, arrange chats via WhatsApp, check out Snapchat, tag photographs, watch videos, search for updates on Instagram and 'message' their friends – using acronyms such as PAW ('parents are watching') and WTTP ('want to trade pictures?') – the minute they wake up, if not throughout the night (that is, if the parent-police haven't switched off the wi-fi), those born before the digital revolution find themselves lagging ignominiously behind. Although the internet groups may not meet face-to-face that often (a teenager's bedroom sometimes offers more potential than going out), it *feels* to them as if they are constantly in one another's company.

Does it matter that this new method of communication has changed lives so quickly that those of us who grew up without it are at a loss to understand its impact? While you are laboriously preparing your shopping list, either on paper ('What's paper, Grandma?') or for the younger at heart online for delivery to your home, your children and grandchildren have contacted friends (although a text can't replace a hug), bought tickets for a gig, listened to music, exchanged selfies, researched homework, streamed the latest movie, booked a nose-piercing or a tattoo appointment, accessed the train timetable, ascertained the price of the newest technology, ordered a pizza, listened to a podcast and, if the worst comes to the very worst, googled hard-core porn.

In their dependence on their technical skills and the speed and volume of internet communication, has the present generation surrendered the ability to think for itself? Without their aptitude can their parents and grandparents, with their engaged thinking that relies on long-term memory, even begin to understand contemporary culture? While previous revolutions in communication – the invention of hieroglyphics and alphabets and the development of the printing press – were accompanied by spiritual revolutions, this has not as yet been the case with the internet which, on the contrary, has provided platforms for bigotry, prejudice, violence, hate, misogyny and grotesque propaganda.

What, if anything, must be done? Confiscate the hardware that grabs the attention only to scatter it? You must be joking! Life would come to an end. Grit your teeth and pay the monthly bill? Suppose the kids were in trouble and needed to contact you urgently, that is exactly what you do. When the instagrammers and tweeters are mugged for their mobiles you are thankful that they escaped with their lives.

Can it be that you are jealous? That you envy a generation with the whole world at its fingertips which, clued up as you may be, you have little chance of accessing. Was it the same when the typewriter was invented? Type 'Remington' or 'Underwood' into Google, throw in the odd 'hashtag' and you might just find out. But what exactly is a hashtag, and if a message reads 'Hashtag me' what on earth do you do?

The hashtag (the # symbol on the far right of the computer keyboard) increases exposure and 'organizes significant words on social media'. It can be used to express emotion, to identify places, brands or events and to connect with other people. The internet is as vast as the universe and already you are out of your depth. Enquiring further, you will learn that a website is 'a location connected to the internet that maintains one or more web pages typically served from a single web domain'. If you say so.

For those of us on the periphery of this brave new world, it is not only the internet that must be mastered but the ubiquitous 'app' – short for 'application' and another name for a computer program – which you install, or which is already installed, on one or other of your 'devices'. These mobile apps, accessed through screen icons, will bring you the latest news, keep your diary, inform you of current weather conditions and allow you to perform specific tasks, such as paying for your parking (assuming you have a car), ordering a takeaway meal or booking a holiday at the press of a button. There is an app for everything and for everything there is an app. There is even an app that helps you to locate your phone should you happen to mislay it, a gadget for bored fathers which connects a baby's bottle to a smartphone and an app powered by artificial intelligence that analyses a couple's language and physiological signs to warn them when they are about to have a row!

While many are of the opinion that computers and mobile phones are changing for ever the way in which our children interact with the world, you can't put the genie back in the bottle. Perhaps the time will come, however, when the human race closes its laptops, puts down its phones, turns its back on the perils of this vast, unregulated experiment on mankind and starts 'talking' to each other.

Hashtag me when that day comes.

3

ON LYING IN THE BATH

I never feel so much myself as when I'm in
a hot bath.

– Sylvia Plath

It has been scientifically proven that a warm bath taken at the
end of the day significantly improves mood and optimism,
benefits attributed to a combination of heat, isolation, body
positioning and comfort, which, according to some scholars,
give rise to pleasurable sensations of security mimicking the
effects of the womb.

While there is a staggering variety of healing, medicinal,
cleansing and therapeutic soaks available – hot water, warm
water, bubble, sitz, saline, mustard, cornstarch, oatmeal, essential oils or other vapours, detox, spa, sponge, disinfectant, clay,
sulphur, etc. etc. – baths have always played an important role
in human health, and there is a bathing tradition in most parts
of the world.

Scandinavians take post-sauna plunges in cool water, while
the renowned love of the Romans for their baths gave rise to
vast complexes, some of which survive, complete with under-
floor heating and a range of water temperatures. Today, however, hot baths, in one guise or another, are largely taken for
relaxation purposes and for getting a bit of time to oneself. On

the issue as to whether they have therapeutic properties the jury is still out. Baths that are too warm put the body under 'heat stress', which is when the internal body-temperature regulation is discombobulated and it doesn't have time to recalibrate: if most of your skin is submerged in scalding water it cannot cool down, and this places a strain on the heart. While Alfred, Lord Tennyson opined that 'It is the height of luxury to sit in a hot bath and read', a hot bath, used as part of 'hyperthermia treatment' as a cure for cancer, is, unfortunately, a myth.

Eighty-five per cent of the world's population live in the driest half of the planet, and 783 million people, one in ten of the world's population, do not have access to clean water – let alone baths and showers – the availability of which is sadly expected to *decrease* in many regions in the future.

The ancient Egyptians, known for their cleanliness, bathed frequently; the Babylonians (before 2000 BC) invented a form of soap; the Greeks – who sometimes had bathrooms – rubbed themselves with olive oil (then rubbed it off with a *strigil*); while the Romans – who took cleanliness seriously – socialized in their public baths which were supplied with clean water brought to the towns via aqueducts. It was not until the fourteenth century that Edward III installed a bathroom in the Palace of Westminster, while his more affluent subjects made do with wooden tubs in their bedrooms (a practice today revived by up-market hotels where claw-footed cast-iron baths sit in the bay windows of 'sea-view' suites). Four centuries later, one William Feetham invented the first modern shower, the use of which did not become common in Britain until the late twentieth century and the benefits of which are hotly debated today.

Surprisingly, twenty-first century research on water efficiency suggests that baths could be more eco-friendly than showers, an equivocal statement that can easily be misunderstood. While it is true that 'power showers' can use more water than a bath, most showers use significantly less. The average hot-water consumption of an eight-minute shower is 62 litres (while some use up to 136 litres), compared with the 80 litres that is run into the average bath.

Those of us who are lucky enough to have unlimited access to water at the turn of a tap are neatly divided into bathers and showerers. Both parties are equally vociferous and defensive about their preferences. The rational arguments in support of their choices are about fifty–fifty. While those who shower invoke speed of action, conservation of water, hygiene and the feelings of physical well-being generated by five minutes under a deluge, the bathers – who feel about a bath in much the same way that religious people feel about holy water – insist that apart from getting them clean a bath, if it is generous enough and at the correct temperature, is conducive to meditation and invention.

Although, to the best of my knowledge, no comparative studies have been carried out, writers are more likely to languish in the warm, womb-like harbour of the bath to get the ideas flowing than to submit to the efficient brutality of the rain-shower. In the embrace of the soothing bath water, which – topping up as necessary – we are reluctant to leave, we polish our plots, fashion our novels, complete our short stories, plan our successes, assuage our disappointments. From within this daily bastion there is little of which, as far as writing is concerned, we are not capable. As the water cools and ideas for plays and sketches, for songs and poems, for articles and essays and the future of our careers proliferate, we realize, with regret, that the overflow is gurgling and that the moment has come to get out.

What is it with baths, the benefits of which are traditionally focused on psychological relaxation and questionable panaceas for specific conditions? While bathing habits vary, baths that are too warm have been targeted as being not particularly good for you, but the fact that a warm bath – preferably taken at the end of the day – has been shown to improve one's mood is attributed to a combination of bodily comfort, warmth, isolation and positioning. As far as I am aware, no studies have been done on the benefits of the bath to the writer who may step into the tub without an idea in his or her head and emerge from its inspirational waters much, much later (*pace* the apparent harmful side-effects), his or her brain reeling with chapters completed, plot lines resolved and new ideas competing for head space. While some authorities associate the horizontal position we assume when bathing with the warm, liquid conditions of the womb, others assume that this gives the bathers (as distinct from the showerers enjoying their masochistic downpours) a sensation of security. Others suggest that the heat generated by a hot bath provides the equivalent of a 'hot pack' that increases the temperature of aching muscles, blocks pain sensors and produces relief.

A good night's sleep is associated with a host of health benefits from a strengthening of the immune system to faster pain recovery, and what better place is there to achieve this than through the night-time bath? With all due respect to the pundits, however, I beg to differ. Massively overheated through a hot bath at night, I find myself 'revved up' rather than 'chilled out' and as far as sleep is concerned might not have bothered going to bed. Anecdotally a warm bath is said to soothe arthritic pain and can abort the common cold. There is as yet no paper written about the effect of a bath on the creative brain.

It was during the French Revolution in 1789 that Jean-Paul Marat, a revolutionary martyr who suffered from a debilitating skin condition, was brutally murdered in his medicinal bath by Charlotte Corday, a Royalist sympathizer. His bloody and unfortunate end was immortalized by the artist Jacques-Louis David, whose graphic depiction of the scene is one of the most haunting images ever to be captured in oils.

Bathing has its dangers, and in the USA, according to statistics, someone drowns in a bath nearly every day, 90 per cent of whom are children. William Howard Taft, the heaviest US president at 332 pounds, not only became stuck in the White House bath but caused a flood by displacing water in the tub of a New Jersey hotel. In our own time Jim Morrison, the lead singer of the rock band The Doors and known for drug and alcohol abuse, was found dead in his Paris bath. He was assumed to have died from heart failure. Singer Whitney Houston suffered a similar watery fate, aided and abetted by overdosing on barbiturates, as did the French pop idol Claude François who in 1978 tried to fix a broken light bulb while standing in a water-filled bath.

An aficionado of the hot bath, I prefer to align myself with the sixteenth-century Greek polymath Archimedes, who discovered the physics of displacement while soaking in his bathtub. He noticed that the water into which he had stepped had risen and realized that the volume of water displaced was an exact measure of the portion of his body that was submerged. He aligned this to measuring the volume of all kinds of objects in the same way. As the legend goes, so eager was Archimedes to share this discovery that he leaped out of the bath and ran naked through the streets of Syracuse proclaiming 'Eureka, Eureka' – 'I have found it, I have found it'. When he was asked by the Emperor to tell him whether or not the royal crown was made of pure gold, Archimedes measured its volume by means of 'water displacement' and compared it to the volume of an equal weight of gold known to be pure. The differences indicated that the crown had some lighter material beneath the gold, and life for the renowned mathematician, who went on to make many more scientific contributions (whether his Eureka moment was one of them is open to conjecture), was never the same again. It's a good story anyway!

While I do not presume to equate myself with Archimedes, I can report, with hand on heart, that many of my ideas, plots and solutions to ideas and plots have arisen – necessitating immediate transfer to sodden notepad or memory – while chilling out in the relaxing waters of a piping-hot bath. Although today my bathtub is kitted out with an ingenious contraption which, with the help of a battery, lowers and raises my body into the water, I cannot imagine life without my daily, relaxing, steaming, soothing and inspirational fix.

4

IN SEARCH OF LOST TIME

All's well that ends well.
– William Shakespeare

The wind blows, a deadline looms, all's right with the world until the printer has a hissy-fit and declares that there is, in its entrails, in the very depths of its being, an unequivocal 'paper jam'. The usual procedures are followed – it is not, after all, the first time it has downed tools – but the message remains: 'PAPER JAM', even when the crumpled copy paper has been removed from its depths and the obstruction is cleared. How can this be? This baby, this efficient workhorse of a printer, is only two years old.

At the same time as you interrupt the flow of your work and wonder – in the absence of any visible obstruction within the entrails of the machine – what is causing the blockage sixteen-year-old Chandra in Mumbai, India, creeps from the mattress on the floor in the eight-foot-square rickety shack that serves as bedroom, kitchen and sitting-room, with a corner for washing, which she shares with her mother, her three sisters and her two brothers. Careful not to waken them, she starts her ablutions taking in her palm water from the bucket she has filled the night before which, accompanied by the appropriate prayer, would lift her mind from the mundane to the sublime, sustain her spirit, as well as her body, imbue her with a positive, optimistic self-image and fit her for the adversity of the day which lay ahead. She does not eat anything. There is nothing to eat. Not even a chapatti. She would skip breakfast and manage till her lunch break, twenty minutes in which to buy her favourite *pav bhaji* – a spicy vegetable curry with a soft bread roll – in the street. What has Chandra's rumbling stomach to do with the printer-jam on a London writer's desk? Time, precious because each one of us has only a limited amount of it, will tell.

Let us say the manufacturer of the recalcitrant printer is Nectarine. It is a tried and tested brand. You have the appropriate contact details and punch in its number on your telephone keypad praying that your call will be answered by a human being. Not a chance.

'Welcome to Nectarine, and thank you for contacting Nectarine support. Did you know that you can also contact us online at www.nectarine.com/uk/totalcare? Calls may be recorded for training and quality purposes. To hear Nectarine's privacy statements please press option 1. For support with PC-related products, including tablets, please press option 2. For support with printers please press option 3. If you are interested in purchasing a product or for service for an existing product please press option 4. To hear these options again please press option 0.'

I press 'zero' then 'three'.

'My name is Raag. How may I help you?'

'My printer has jammed.'

Oh not again! By the time we get to 'Yankee' I am losing my cool.

'Look, could you *please* just put me through to technical support.'

'Can I have the first line of your address?"

I supply it.

'Thank you. And what is the postcode?'

The information is followed by silence, then 'Your printer is out of warranty.'

'Yes, I know.'

'That will be eighteen pounds.'

'OK.'

'What card would you like to pay with?'

The full name 'as it appears on the card', 'the long number on the front of the card', 'the start date', 'the expiry date' and the 'security number on the back of the card' are disclosed. I pray this will not result in cybercrime.

'Thank you. That has gone through. Is there anything else I can help you with?'

'Yes. My printer has jammed. I have been on the telephone for ten minutes, listened to umpteen announcements and spoken to two people. I would like to be put through to technical support.'

'I will do that for you now, ma'am. The line will go quiet, but please do not hang up. Have a nice day.'

I seethe while the line goes quiet and am about to hang up.

'Hallo. My name is Bivu. How may I help you?'

'My printer has jammed.'

'Can you please give me your name?'

We go through the pilot's code from R to Y.

'May I please have the first line of your address?'

'Look, you are the third person I have spoken to . . .'

'When did you purchase your printer? Your printer is out of warranty...' And on it goes. I speak to Maisa and to Geon who is very sorry but he only deals with inkjet printers and mine is a laserjet. He will transfer me to the appropriate technical support who will be able to help me and, as I feel my blood about to boil, urges me to have a nice day and not to hang up as the line goes quiet. Two full minutes later Chandra picks up the call. After only a few hours' sleep and no breakfast she is still tired. She is thinking about her boy-friend of whom her mother does not approve. She cannot discuss him with her father. Her father is in gaol. The line breaks up, and I can hardly hear her as the words 'name', 'model number' and 'what is the problem?' bounce jerkily back and forth in the ether between London and Mumbai. Losing my rag, near to tears of frustration – I will never buy another Nectarine product – and ashamed of myself I shout the required information into the receiver, repeating the mantra for the umpteenth time.

"I . . . help . . . bloggle, bloggle . . . bloggle" Chandra's voice turns into a stream of gobbledegook which gets lost some-where over the Indian Ocean.

'I can't hear you.'

'Bloggle, bloggle . . . better?'

'Yes. No . . .'

'. . . Very bad line. There . . . distortion. If . . . bloggle . . . your telephone number I will . . . bloggle you back.'

If you believe that you believe anything. Forty-five minutes and four different 'Nectarines' and I have not yet got round to discussing the paper jam. I replace my receiver. The telephone rings almost immediately.

'You are speaking to Chandra.'

The voice is clear!

'Can you hear me, ma'am?' Chandra was thinking of her *pav bhaji* and whether she would dare take her boyfriend's hand. 'There is a problem with your printer, ma'am?'

'It says "paper jam",' I say weakly. 'There *is* no paper jam.'

'I can help you with that.'

Following Chandra's crystal-clear instructions I crawl round to the back of the printer and disconnect the mains, repowering the printer, as directed, after two minutes. 'PAPER JAM,' it announces on screen once more. I disconnect the printer USB cable from the computer. 'PAPER JAM,' it repeats.

'When did you last change the cartridge, ma'am?' Chandra asks. 'Can you tell me if it is a genuine Nectarine cartridge? Do you have the old cartridge? What I want you to do for me, ma'am, is to insert the old cartridge into the printer and try once more to print.'

'Paper jam.'

'Your printer is broken.'

'I've only had it two years!'

There is an audible yawn from Chandra who has already dealt with twenty-five calls and a steady stream of bad language, to which she is accustomed, from frustrated customers. She checks her watch. It is nowhere near lunchtime.

'Are you telling me that I have to buy a *new* printer?'

'I can help you with that. I am going to transfer you now to Sales. Thank you for calling Nectarine Support. The line will go dead for a few minutes, but . . .'

I am not proud of myself for slamming down the receiver. I have wasted the entire morning. How many more people would I have to speak to? Why would I buy a Nectarine product again?

I call my computer guru, by whom I swear. He is busy with clients all day. We cyber ignorami are a pathetic bunch. When he finally rings the doorbell – two hours after the appointed time as he had an unexpectedly long job before getting to me – I am eating dinner. I put down my knife and fork and let my meal grow cold while I accompany him to the malfunctioning printer.

'What's the problem?' His voice is cheery.

'Paper jam,' I say weakly.

He reads the offending message on the display, opens the appropriate flap of the printer, removes the cartridge, flicks up the black roller above it and, looking sombre, selects a tweezer-like gadget from his neatly packed tool-kit.

Approaching the printer once more, and with the dexterity of a surgeon removing an inflamed appendix, he scrabbles into its depths and, withdrawing the tweezers triumphantly, holds aloft a chewed-up elastic-band.

'How did that get in there?'

I have no idea.

The 'PAPER JAM' message has disappeared.

Halleluja. We are back in business.

5

A WALK IN
THE PARK

> People seem to think that there is something
> inherently noble and virtuous in the desire to go for
> a walk. Anyone thus desirous feels that he has a right
> to impose his will on whomever he sees comfortably
> settled in an armchair, reading.

– Max Beerbohm

Walking is not only one of the easiest ways to get fit and ideal for people of all ages but, like lying in a hot bath, it frees the mind. I am not talking here about exercise – which entails walking boots, granola bars, sunscreen, a backpack and the latest Fitbit, with the intention of raising your heart rate and breaking out into a sweat – but exertion of moderate intensity, punctuated by frequent hiatuses for standing and staring, which can be little faster than a stroll. A pair of comfortable shoes or trainers is all the equipment you need.

The *flâneur*, meanderer or promenader of French nineteenth-century literature and important symbol for scholars, artists and writers, was a man of leisure, an idler, an urban explorer and a connoisseur of the street. There was nothing mindless or lazy about those whose *flânerie* led them to a rich understanding of the landscape they encountered. In the words of Baudelaire, 'to see the world, to be at the centre of the world, and yet to remain hidden from the world...The spectator is a prince who everywhere rejoices in his incognito.'

While Baudelaire's *flâneur* was absorbed by the kaleidoscopic experience of the metropolis, my own curiosity and laziness, my personal 'gastronomy of the eye', takes me only across the road from where I live to the perennial delights of Regent's Park, one of the most beautiful pleasure grounds of any capital city, a curious development whose history can be traced back through seven centuries, before Nash and his patron the Prince Regent laid it out as the first of the improvements they had planned for London. Although it is a residential area, half of its 550 acres were left as parkland. Contrary to received opinion, however, architect John Nash did not have the good of the masses at heart. His idea was that the park should be an exclusive preserve for the sole use of the occupants of the splendid villas that surrounded it and in particular for the Prince Regent who was to have a palace at its centre. It was not until a century later that the park was opened up for the enjoyment of all. The terraces that surround it are made up of tall, narrow houses. While their original interiors are similar to those of many other nineteenth-century dwellings, their neoclassical façades, with their Doric columns and friezes, are iced with stucco and designed to appeal to the lofty aspirations of anyone who could afford them and who wanted a statement home from which they could hear the quack of the ducks in the duck pond. The plan of the park is essentially a pair of concentric circles – which bamboozle visitors trying to find their way to the London Business College or to Baker

Street Station – instead of the gridiron pattern on which London had developed throughout the eighteenth century. Originally the park was a part of the Middlesex Forest: 'a great forest with wooded glades and lairs of wild beasts, deer both red and fallow, wild bulls and boars'[1] of which Samuel Pepys wrote, 'Then we went abroad to Marrow-bone and there walked in the garden, the first time I was ever there and a pretty place it is.'

While the origins of Regent's Park can be traced back to King Henry VIII, who used it as a hunting ground, history is not my strong point, and as I take my daily *flânerie* through the imposing gates of Queen Mary's Gardens to the avenues of trees, the lakes, the formal gardens and the fountains, I am more interested in the contemporary kaleidoscope of visitors who frequent the park at different times of day and throughout the year. The massed roses with their evocative names – Ingrid Bergman, Song and Dance, Nostalgia and Belle Epoque – and the enticing snippets of snatched conversation interest me more than the fact that I am strolling through the past.

For Virginia Woolf, as for many writers, creation and walking were inseparable. Putting one foot in front of the other freed her mind and gave her time to think. When she was ill and unable to leave the house, she imagined herself into walking on the slopes of the Ouse valley or on the Sussex Downs and made up stories about the triumphs and disappointments of human life.

A park is many things to many people. Regent's Park is no exception. Visitors traverse it, from different points of entry,

1. William Fitzstephen's description of London in Sir Frank Stenton's *Norman London*, Historical Association, London, 1934.

throughout the year. It caters for all ages and, like a magnet, attracts sightseers from every corner of the globe, providing physical and spiritual respite from the hullabaloo of quotidian life. Its open spaces, its lakes, its birds, its trees and flowers are balm to the overtaxed mind. It is hardly surprising that in all weathers, and at any time of day, a variety of dress can be seen and many nationalities encountered. Pinpointing the ethnicity of the passers-by by their clothes and their accents is one of the many games that I play with myself on my solitary excursions.

While cycling and skating in the park is permitted in some areas, walking is the activity of choice. In the mornings, commuters, ears clamped to smartphones or headsets, lap-tops and lunches in their briefcases, stride purposefully to work: nurses and hedge-fund managers, security guards and CEOs? While it's amusing to try to guess what brings them here you'll never know. Latecomers move more leisurely, stop to rest on one of the many benches dedicated to the memory of the deceased, 'who so loved this park', as they make their way to the Regent's Bar and Kitchen, the Smokehouse or the Honest Sausage for refreshment. In summer, having staked their territorial claims, visitors lay out picnics on the grass – sandwiches, falafel, spring rolls, samosas –an international kaleidoscope of *déjeuners sur l'herbe*. Children, accompanied by proud parents, come out at weekends and school holidays. New doll's prams and pristine scooters are the harbingers of Christmas, while the many densely bushed nooks and crannies furnish hideaways for couples who communicate with each other in the secret language of love.

In permitted areas, every breed of dog may be seen from dawn till dusk when the park closes, chasing balls and sticks and forming canine associations. While small boys and boisterous girls enjoy the swings and slides and sandpits in the play areas, serious joggers and runners of all ages – with their ubiquitous bottles of water – take their dedicated exercise. Chinese people practise the graceful art of t'ai chi, keep-fitters shadow their personal trainers and bird-watchers keep their eyes peeled for tufted ducks, mute swans, whoopies, reed-warblers, tree pipits and yellow grebes. Although cyclists are banned from many areas, bicycles have recently been permitted on the Broadwalk, and the Inner and Outer Circles provide circuits which are also enjoyed by those with disabilities, with their carers or other associates, on tricycles for two. In the park itself self-conscious brides, clutching colourful bouquets and shivering in flimsy dresses or elegant saris, hitch up their skirts to ascend the wooden bridges over the shallow water or, watched by proud parents, clutch newly minted bridegrooms as they are captured on video beneath the willow trees. Nearby, in Queen Mary's Gardens, less animated groups, intoning prayers in tongues, assemble to scatter the ashes of their loved ones.

Another park attraction is the Zoological Society of London –more commonly known as the London Zoo – with its lemurs, polar bears and giant pandas, from where animal cries fill the morning air and outside which there is a permanent queue, hefty entrance fees notwithstanding. While the Colosseum and the Diorama – early versions of the cinema – no longer exist, the Open Air Theatre offers Shakespeare and Sondheim to locals and tourists come rain or shine. On a more sombre note, the original bandstand – transferred from Richmond to Regent's Park – was targeted by the IRA who on 20 July 1982 detonated a bomb beneath it, killing seven men of the Royal Greenjackets.

A happier musical association is with the composer Ralph Vaughan Williams, who lived in the park in the years preceding his death in 1958, and Richard Wagner, who on his visits to London fed the ducks from Hanover Bridge and admired the swans on the lake. Other literary names associated with the park are Charles Dickens, H.G. Wells, George Eliot and Charles Darwin.

For many years Regent's Park has been administered by the Department of Culture, Media and Sport. It is now, however – to the chagrin of its residents who deplore the cacophony emanating from loudspeakers and the crowds and traffic which ensue – becoming more commercially orientated. Annual events are the Frieze Art Fair, with its displays of photography and contemporary exhibits, and Frieze Masters – showcasing Old Masters – as well as Taste of London, the 'World's Greatest Restaurant Festival' attended by 'the world's greatest chefs'. The intention of the powers-that-be is to turn the Royal Parks into charitable corporations similar to those administering the Royal Palaces. The proposed 'attractions', together with the all-weather tennis courts, boating lakes and fund-raising walks, reinforce the idea that the park today is neither the park that Nash envisaged nor that which opened to the public in 1835. Over time, several of the original buildings have been lost, and there have been many changes of use. The demand that the park increase its revenue is at times incompatible with its original purpose, which stated that it was to be 'a refuge from the pressures of the modern world and a place of physical and spiritual recreation'.

While Regent's Park, a Mecca for locals and tourists alike, is used as a shortcut to work for some, for others it is a place to relax, to exercise and to inhale the fresh air. For the writer, however, it is a rich seam to be mined. As she weaves a path through the roses she neither captures their heady blooms on her iPhone or tablet nor coaxes the tame squirrels to quaintly pose for her. She does not take photographs, refuses to walk anywhere with her head in a travel guide and, unable to capture an emotion on a machine, does not carry a camera. Her recording device is in her head. As she makes her way along the paths, among the pallid Japanese in their ubiquitous sunhats, couples in identical Barbours, illicit lovers, Middle Eastern matrons trailing darkly in the wake of their men, sun-kissed girls with sun-kissed legs, *soignée* French and pashmina-wearing Italians, bored fathers, dedicated runners, city traders, proud parents with the latest in baby-buggies, anxious grandmothers with toddlers, multiracial school kids, lonely widows and widowers, foreigners with maps, birdwatchers with notebooks, artists with easels, vagabonds with beer cans and hedonists with bared chests, she overhears enticing snippets of conversation which fertilize the half-formed ideas in her head. 'He went very quickly in the end . . .' A brother, a father, a canary? 'When I got home there was this voicemail . . .' 'I said why don't you take the train?' 'Ten fish fingers for a pound!'

Regent's Park attracts millions of visitors each year. It is a magnet for ramblers and perfect for contemplation, for the aimless saunterer with no specific goal. The nature of the flâneuse is to be invisible, to immerse herself in the crowd, to be at the centre of everything yet to remain hidden. While the park is many things to many people, if you have eyes with which to see it, if what you are searching for is experience rather than knowledge, all of life is there.

While the Outer Circle attracts a number of racing cyclists who use it as a training area, Transport for London has plans to transform the quiet environ into a 'cycle super-highway'. This, together with suggestions for park-gate closures at certain times of day, is of great concern to those who fear that their enjoyment of the historic streetscape will be compromised.

On the vexed question of how the Regent's Park – together with the other Royal Parks – will look, feel and operate as 'dedicated environments for cycling enthusiasts' rather than for the benefit of residents, visitors and all who enjoy it the jury is still out.

6

HOUSEHOLD GODS

He must have furniture gleaming with gold
vessels and antique silver plate wrought by famous
artists.

– Seneca

We all, no matter how ascetic, have our *lares* and *penates* with
which we surround ourselves and which define our status, our
gender and our place in society. This ephemera provides the
rich pickings – apart from our loved ones and our animals –
from which we would select items to grab were our habitats to
be threatened by fire or insurrection.

In the 1930s, in suburban parlours or 'drawing-rooms' – as
they were pretentiously referred to – would frequently be
found a collection of artefacts that children were not permitted
to touch. On the ubiquitous baby-grand piano (an upright in
the day nursery, ruled over by 'nannie', sufficed for painful
renderings of *Für Elise*) would stand silver photograph frames
of deceased relatives in unfamiliar clothes with unfamiliar
names, while on nests of tables, put to use when there were
visitors, or on the mantelpiece above the Magicoal (a gas or
electric fire purporting to burn solid fuel) might be found
carved ivories four or five inches high depicting peasant
women and fishermen with finely wrought fishing-rods; silver

bon-bon dishes filled – on 'bridge' days – with minuscule dragées and delicately tinted sugared almonds; French horses and riders; facsimiles of Nijinsky, the Russian ballet dancer, in gold and enamel; terracotta violin players; Art Deco statuettes of curly-haired children clutching teddy-bears seated eternally upon marble chairs; dancing couples with pointed toes (Pierrot and Pierrette, tragic lovers, doomed never to come together) in elaborately detailed costumes; and chrome trays from the Czech Republic, engraved with leaping ebony lionesses, for serving the ubiquitous Martinis. Such collections represented a middle-class substitute for living, as if, by seeking to immerse themselves in a timeless world of objects and ritual, pre-war adults hoped to reinvent the one they inhabited, soon to be blown apart.

It was not only the ornaments which in those days were not allowed to be handled. Life for children was hedged about with incomprehensible restrictions and paternalistic edicts which were none the less obeyed. In many families it was as much as their lives were worth for children to question an adult decree or voice a contrary opinion. It is hardly surprising that today's older generation look on with amazement, and not a little envy, at their grandchildren. Shod in the universal trainers rather than the ubiquitous Start-Rite shoes once *de rigueur*, they are encouraged not only to participate in adult conversation but both to interrupt it and to 'answer back' as they sit not round mahogany tables over meat and two veg which it was obligatory to finish, leaving a clean plate, but on bar-stools in 'kitchen-diners' where takeaways from cardboard boxes are consumed more with fingers than with cutlery. The *lares* and *penates* of such a 'modern' family no longer consist of facsimiles of ballet dancers, ivory fishermen, cherished dolls' houses nor Hornby trains but of smartphones and iPads addiction to which has subsumed the long-forgotten delights of construction sets such as Meccano and board games such as Ludo and Snakes and Ladders, which, in the absence of television, once whiled away the twilight hours.

Plus ça change plus c'est la même chose! Nonsense. Today is quite another world which the elderly – many of whom are still able to function quite nicely without wi-fi or the internet – look upon with wonder.

The pace of change is exponential. How did we manage without Post-It notes, fish-fingers, false eyelashes and ring-pulls, without bar codes, seat-belts and microwave ovens, the magic of which stemmed directly from the development of radar by Britain during the Second World War? Gone are the days when the milkman, on his daily round, left pints of milk and gills of Jersey cream (no worries then about cholesterol) on the doorstep in response to notes rolled up and inserted into yesterday's glass bottles; when the progress of his blinkered nag was followed by diligent gardeners with shovels? Who can remember the red-eyed hauliers lugging hundredweight bags of coal and coke on their backs which they would empty into our cellars, as the tree-lined streets echoed with reverberating cries of 'Sackoal!'

Apart from enduring two world wars, the coldest winter since records began and the Great Depression with its ensuing Stock Exchange Crash, the third decade of the twentieth century (into the last knockings of which I was born) and subsequent decades saw innovations that transformed housework and saved lives. While the Victorians gave us electric power and light, the telephone, radio, photography, cars and railways, they also generated many of the ideas – from Darwinism and Communism to the Arts and Crafts Movement – that changed twentieth-century thinking. After the First World War, which preceded 'my' war in 1939 and killed 10 million young men, domestic and social life changed for ever. Housemaids, hitherto responsible for cleaning the Pierrots and Pierrettes with their feather dusters, became nurses and secretaries, and the liberated 'housewife' had the means to walk away from her china cabinet (in which the heirloom Spode and crystal were intended to endure a whole married life and to be passed on to the next generation) and to express herself differently.

While the washtub, the 'copper', the mangle, the carpet sweeper, the flat-iron and the strong right arm gave way to the electric washing-machine, the vacuum cleaner, the steam iron and the food-mixer; fish-fingers, sliced bread, pop-up toasters, rubber gloves, plastic bags and clingfilm transformed the post-war kitchen, and parking meters, seatbelts, cats'-eyes and supermarket trolleys changed the world outside.

It was not all good, however. Chainsaws became the means for the destruction of the rainforests, 'disposable' products – nappies and paper tissues – polluted the environment and aerosol gases damaged the ozone layer. 'Growth' and the hankering after the latest 'must-haves' became the ailments of our time.

There is no doubt that great technological and scientific strides have been made since the end of the Second World

War, but the rise in the UK of an oligarchy which has priced many indigent citizens out of the housing market, the production of 'high-end' accessories (for which one of the magnets is a waiting-list), which are sold for a king's ransom while the minimum wage remains derisory and food banks are the order of the day, leaves a nasty taste in the mouth.

The red-soled *Louboutins* of footballer's wives, the Patek Philippe watches of the men about town and the sought-after Hermès handbags have become present-day status symbols. Have they also become the *lares* and *penates* which, to our cultural shame, we would rescue from the fire?

7

DEATH AND LIFE

The heart has its reasons of which reason knows
nothing.

– Blaise Pascal

A heart-lung transplant is a major and rarely performed surgical procedure where a person's diseased heart and lungs are
replaced with those of a recently deceased donor. The length
of time spent on the waiting-list can vary, but it can be several
months or even years. Transplant is a major procedure that carries a high risk of complications, some of which can be fatal. The
operation is usually carried out when all other treatment options
have been exhausted and it is thought that the potential benefits
will outweigh the risks.

My interest in organ transplantation started in April 1996
when one Julia Polak placed an advertisement in the *Writers'
Newsletter* inviting authors who were interested in the subject of
heart-lung transplants to contact her. Not surprisingly she was
deluged with replies.

Because several members of my family were in the medical
profession I considered that I was up to the job (whatever it
was), and, luckily, she thought the same. This was the beginning
of not only a professional alliance but of a warm and close
friendship that endured until the death of Dame Professor Julia
Polak, DBE, MD, DSc, FRC, FRCPath, FMedSci, ILT, in 2015,

nineteen years after she received her own heart-lung transplant which was carried out by her colleague Professor Sir Magdi Yacoub, who, ironically, had previously provided her with samples of lung tissue for her laboratory work.

Not much more than five feet tall, a modest, attractive, dynamic and cheery blonde with a serious intellect, a towering scientific mind and a reputation for kindness and concern for others, Dame Julia's story, one of coincidence and courage, was enough to inspire any writer. Its tragic corollary was hard to credit.

Much has been made of the moral and ethical dilemmas that surround heart-lung and other organ transplant surgery. Who most deserves to live, someone whose death is imminent or a patient who stands a better chance of long-term survival? What can be done about the acute shortage of organs that creates such distressing choices?

Julia was born in Buenos Aires from where she progressed from medical school to become Professor of Endocrine Pathology at the Royal Postgraduate Medical School at Hammersmith Hospital (now part of Imperial College), London, where she was made head of department in 1991.

As a young child she had had respiratory difficulties that steadily worsened with age. By the time she was fifty-five her condition was so serious that she could no longer climb the stairs. While she was thought by her colleagues to be suffering from asthma, she was finally diagnosed with pulmonary hypertension, a rare lung condition that affects around one in a million. In a cruel twist of fate this disease, which results in the narrowing of the blood vessels to the lungs, was the very one that Julia had been researching for the past twelve years. She knew better than anyone that her heart was failing, that she was going downhill rapidly and that the prognosis was not good. She was already on a life-support machine when Professor Yacoub persuaded her that her only chance of survival was to have a heart-and-lung transplant, a high-risk procedure with both moral and ethical concerns, such as the inescapable fact that the chance of life came at the expense of someone else's death. She *could* die with the transplant, but she *would* die without it.

In 1995, when suitable replacement organs became available, Professor Yacoub performed a 'domino' transplant in which he replaced Julia's damaged lungs with the matching heart and lungs of a young woman from the Midlands, to whom her relatives had said a poignant farewell.

As in the case of many transplantees, Julia's recovery, aided and abetted by her devoted husband Professor Daniel Catovsky, a fellow Argentinian, was impeded by rejection and infection, but after three months of daily commitment to a punishing lifestyle regime and adherence to a stringent programme of drugs (many of which had distressing side-effects) her condition began to stabilize. Once she was on her feet again she determined to make it her life's work to find an alternative, more reliable solution for patients with incurable end-stage lung disease as well as those with conditions such as cystic fibrosis and brittle-bone disease, which would do away with both the lack of donor organs and the risk of rejection. To this end she redirected her research to 'tissue engineering', a new scientific field in which the aim was to use stem cells, which, if successful, could offset the shortage of donor organs, overcome the problem of rejection and help the body heal itself. She returned to her laboratory determined to take on this new scientific challenge, and to become one of the longest surviving heart-lung transplant patients in Britain.

Despite facing multiple setbacks, Julia used the gift of the extra years of life she had been granted to help create a future where patients with similar conditions to her own could be helped with injection or implantation of healthy tissue grown from their own cells. She devoted herself to 'regenerative medicine', a new scientific field aimed at the development of ambulatory, bio-artificial lungs to alleviate the suffering of patients afflicted with end-stage lung disorder and looked forward to the day when diseased or damaged body parts would be able to be replaced without the need for surgery.

In 1999 Julia set up the Imperial College Tissue Engineering/Regenerative Medicine Centre, devoted to growing new organs from stem cells, and contributed in helping the college to develop as a place devoted to world-class science, teaching and clinical advances. In 2003 she was honoured in the Queen's Birthday list for her services to medicine and was made Dame Commander of the British Empire. At the investiture Professor Leszek Borysiewicz, then principal of Imperial College Faculty of Medicine, commented, 'This is great news for Julia. She has to her name fantastic scientific achievements and has contributed enormously in helping Imperial develop as a place renowned for world-class science, teaching and clinical advances.'

My role in Julia's story was to write a fund-and-awareness-raising play, *Change of Heart*, about the ethics of playing God and the practical and emotional impact of transplant, in which a cosmopolitan team of doctors is faced with a choice between saving the life of a high-profile medical colleague or that of a teenage girl, the daughter of a television celebrity, both of whom were languishing on the waiting-list. The play had its world première at the New End Theatre, London, where it was warmly received and achieved some positive notices. Reviews said, 'This is dramatic gold'; 'This gripping play examines the complexities of human relationships in a life-threatening situation and poses moral and ethical questions not often heard on stage'; 'This is a moving and thought-provoking play which does not pull its punches'; and 'Contagious entertainment which could have theatregoers waiting on a trolley in a corridor the remainder of the winter.'

The success of the play – in which the late Sir Laurence Olivier's daughter Julie-Kate Olivier played the lead – and my continuing friendship with Julia encouraged me to reprise her story in an equally well-received novel, *Intensive Care*, based on her remarkable life, copies of which the indomitable Julia bullied everyone who crossed her path into buying to raise money for the Julia Polak Research Trust she had set up.

Mother of three, happily married and supported in her career by Daniel, Julia was the author of some 1,000 original papers, one of the most widely cited researchers in her field, and was the European Editor of the journal *Tissue Engineering*. This extraordinary woman was renowned not only for her pioneering work in medicine but for her expertise in tango, her lemon mousse – she was a fantastic cook – and for her warmth, generosity and modesty. In a unique corollary to her transplant, she presented her own diseased lungs in a Powerpoint presentation to a packed audience of incredulous and moist-eyed medical students.

Julia's remarkable story, however, did not end with her death in August 2015, at the age of seventy-five, while still engaged in research to alleviate the suffering of countless patients afflicted with end-stage lung disease. Three years before her demise, her only daughter Marina, a criminal defence lawyer, was knocked down on her way to work by a speeding motorcyclist and was mortally wounded. The devastating news, brought to Julia in the midst of delivering a lecture, was the *coup de grâce* for someone who had known so much suffering. It was only partly mitigated by the fact that, inspired by her mother's extraordinary story and her courage and without telling her, Marina had registered as an organ donor and, thanks to her altruism, four strangers received the 'gift of life'. Thus, if poignantly, the wheel had turned full circle.

8

FRIENDSHIP

Piglet sidled up to Pooh from behind. 'Pooh!'
he whispered.
    'Yes, Piglet?'
    'Nothing,' said Piglet, taking Pooh's paw.
'I just wanted to be sure of you.'

– A.A. Milne

Friendship, 'the supreme human relationship' according to Aristotle and widely discussed by Plato and the Stoics, is life-enhancing. Engaging in activities with like-minded friends intensifies pleasure, increases self-esteem, leads people to share strong interpersonal ties and enables them to feel more at one with themselves. Increasing longevity means deeper friend-ships – flesh and blood not Facebook – which are both good and necessary for human beings. Friendship is part of the glue that holds society together, and, all other things being equal, having strong social connections is the precursor to a happy life. Contentment is good for our health and for our relation-ships. Cheerful people are more likely to marry or to form good partnerships. They are more productive at work, have a greater number of friends, cope better with stress and trauma, are more creative, live longer and are less likely to get sick. Having some-one in whom we can confide and who will support us when we are down is the key to happiness.

In the words of Samuel Johnson, 'If a man does not make new acquaintances as he advances through life, he will soon find himself alone.'

While it is true that genetics have a role to play, people tend to get happier with age and none more so than those who have invested time and effort in forging friendships. Although older adults prefer familiar and established relationships, new friendships can be made throughout life. Interaction with others, among older people with declining health, shows improved psychological well-being.

True friendship develops when two people are able to trust one another with their innermost thoughts and feelings without fear of ridicule. A friend can be a relative, a school or college pal, a work colleague or any other person for whom feelings of affection are mutual: someone who knows all about you but still loves you. It is not a lack of love but a lack of friendship between couples that makes for miserable marriages. The crucial point about friendship is endurance. True friends are there for you whatever and whenever, and today's greater longevity means deeper friendships, although the lives of those who have reached the top of their professions but who are poor team players can sometimes be lonely.

While our first interaction is with our parents, no matter how much we love them, how much we 'get on' with them, there will almost always be a generational barrier. They sing from a different song sheet and cannot, by definition, be our 'friends'. Friendship is about communication, and the secret thoughts and hopes of parents cannot, by their very nature, be shared with children and vice versa. A true friend, and one to be cherished, is someone to whom you can reveal your grief, joys and fears, someone to whom you can open up in the knowledge that no matter what secrets, what hopes and desires you confess to they will not tread on your dreams. Like a good physician, a true friend knows you intimately, and when you ask for his or her advice there is no danger that your friend will cure the disease but kill the patient. C.S. Lewis suggested that friendship is born the moment when one person says to another, 'What! You too? I thought I was the only one.' As A.A. Milne said, 'You can't stay in your corner of the Forest waiting for others to come to you. You have to go to them sometimes.'

Friendship generally flourishes between people of roughly the same age and mind-set. It is a relationship of mutual affection and a stronger form of interpersonal bond than mere association. While there is no hard-and-fast rule, no blueprint for friendship, bonds tend to be formed between people of similar background, occupations or interests. The characteristics of a close affinity between two people are affection, sympathy, empathy, honesty, altruism, mutual understanding, compassion, enjoyment of each other's company and the freedom to express one's feelings and, most importantly, one's failures without fear of judgement. People who form close associations with others tend to be happier than those who do not. The absence of friends can be emotionally damaging. Bonds are often formed between parental and pair bonding, and friends can be the most important component in the emotional life of the adolescent. These bonds are frequently more powerful than any subsequent relationships.

In the nursery friendships are based on the sharing of toys and the carrying out of activities together. Although sharing can be difficult, young children are more likely to be generous with someone they regard as their 'best friend'. Observing little ones in playgroups often gives an indication of how they are likely to interact with adults in later life. As they mature, children become more aware of other children, begin to see one another's point of view and to participate in group activities. They also learn to cope with rejection. Establishing good relationships with a friend at a very young age is not only touching to observe but helps children integrate into society later on. While they value those with similar attitudes and interests, pre-school children often find it less easy to cope with friendships that involve conflict, dominance, rivalry and other negative features.

Empathy and problem-sharing are often acted out in childhood, and adolescent friendships are generally stronger and longer lasting than those formed earlier. Antisocial behaviour – stealing, fighting and truancy – is often influenced by friends who do not fit in at school.

In the transition from adolescence to adulthood, life events – marriage, parenthood and career development – can compromise friendship. Married or cohabiting couples tend to have an average of only two close friends. It can be hard to form relationships in the competitive atmosphere of the workplace, where true feelings may be hidden amid difficulties in opening up to colleagues.

In later life, as family and vocational responsibilities recede and health deteriorates, fewer new friendships are formed and the old ones assume greater importance. Older people who remain in contact with longstanding friends show improved psychological well-being. New friendships tend to be formed with people whose age, sex, race, ethnicity and values are similar to their own. Few of the elderly form new friendships with those of the opposite sex, and secondary friendships – usually between women – are often formed at adult-education classes, over lunch or at the bridge or bingo table.

Friendships founder for many reasons. They may end through disagreement, fade away as a result of acceptance of one or the other into a new social group or as a consequence of divorce when loyalties are divided. Sometimes, as friends retire and move home, the reasons are geographical. While digital technology has made distance less of an obstacle, many elderly people have not got their heads round the internet, and, in the absence of face-to-face encounters, bonds, that were once close may wither and die.

In Ancient Greece *philos* referred both to a friend and a lover, which could give rise to misunderstanding. In some Asian cultures to be someone's 'best friend' is considered an honour, and it is regarded as a connection that is usually never broken until one or other moves away or leaves the country. In Islamic society, where men often hold hands as a sign of friendship, friendship is known as 'companionship' or *ashab*, and forgiveness regarding mistakes and loyalty between friends is emphasized. 'Love for the sake of Allah' is considered to be a relationship of the highest significance between two human beings. In some parts of the Middle and Near East friendship is more demanding; friends are people who respect each other, regardless of their shortcomings, and who will make personal sacrifices in order to help one another. Many Arab peoples regard friendship with the utmost gravity and consider personal attributes, such as social influence and the nature of someone's character, before committing to such a relationship.

In Russia during the Soviet period conditions made it difficult for people to form friendships. Confiding in another person carried the risk of being reported to the state. Young adults today, however, tend to use a more realistic approach in order to get ahead in their studies, as well as in the workplace, and this can affect their friendships.

Germans, typically, have relatively few friends, although friendships may last a lifetime and loyalty is held in high regard. A strong distinction is drawn between 'friends' and co-workers, neighbours and others. Transition from the role of associate to friend can take months or years and is relatively rare.

In the USA – where it is the fashion among the young to exchange friendship bracelets – the term 'friendship' is applied to relationships that elsewhere in the world would be categorized as 'acquaintanceship'; friendships tend to be superficial, short-lived and limited in intimacy, rather than lifelong exchanges of solidarity and moral and emotional support. While people might refer to those with whom they are especially close as their 'best friends', these tend to be individuals whom they encounter fairly often but with whom they frequently lose touch. Many Americans have no close confidants, a situation compounded by the high rate of divorce when friends tend to side with one or other of the feuding parties. The advance of social media has also been blamed for the decline of face-to-face friendship and makes emotional attachment harder to achieve.

Throughout history, literature and the arts – David and Jonathan in the Old Testament, Horatio and Hamlet at Shakespeare's court of Denmark, Don Quixote and Sancho Panza in Cervantes' novel, Elizabeth Bennett and Charlotte Lucas in *Pride and Prejudice*, Bob Hope and Bing Crosby in the 'Road' movies, to film actors George Clooney and Brad Pitt – famous friendships, many of them unlikely, abound.

The crucial point about friendship is its endurance. True friends are always there for one another, and today's greater longevity means that deeper relationships can be formed. No matter how wealthy you are, a sixty-year-old friendship cannot be bought.

'Those friends thou hast, and their adoption tried, / Grapple them to thy side with hoops of steel . . .' Shakespeare, as usual, has the last word.

9

LOVE

How do I love thee? Let me count the ways.
I love thee to the depth and breadth and height
My soul can reach, when feeling out of sight
For the ends of being and ideal grace.
I love thee to the level of every day's
Most quiet need, by sun and candle-light.
I love thee freely, as men strive for right . . .

– Elizabeth Barrett Browning

In Plato's *Symposium* Aristophanes declares that the 'loved one' is our long-lost 'other half' to whose body our own had originally been joined. When Elizabeth Barrett declared her love for Robert Browning in *Sonnets from the Portuguese* she was in the grip of a *coup de foudre* or 'thunderbolt', a seminal instance of love at first sight. Other authors have declared that we are not wholly alive until we have loved and experienced the distressing euphoria, sleeplessness, racing heart, loss of appetite and mood swings that parallel the behaviour of the drug addict.

While love can take many guises and has several gradations, ranging from affection to sensations of warmth, tenderness, kindness, devotion, sentiment, attachment and intimacy, few have managed to convey the depths of feeling of one human being for another than the nineteenth-century poet manages to do in a fourteen-line sonnet.

She was reluctant to publish her poetry owing to its intimate nature, until Robert Browning, to whom the poems were addressed, convinced her of their importance. To protect her privacy Elizabeth called the poems *The Sonnets from the Portuguese* in order to create the impression that she had merely translated them, rather than written them herself, while the choice of title is thought to have been inspired by Browning's affectionate nickname for her, 'my little Portuguese'.

Although many novelists, wordsmiths and playwrights have tried, and many have succeeded, most of us would be hard put to convey to the proverbial 'man from Mars' precisely what is meant by the word 'love'. Like many other sicknesses, the sensation of being in love is impossible to define but easy to recognize. In common with the drug addict the lover will have mood swings and, bouncing between euphoria and despondency, experience loss of appetite and tachycardia and suffer anxiety and panic attacks as well as feelings of desolation. Where 'love sickness' is concerned, you will know when you've got it and soon realize that it is a condition for which there is no known panacea.

Many different theories attempt to explain the true nature and function of love. Trying to describe it to the 'man in the street' is like attempting to convey the taste of roast chicken to a vegan or the colours of the rainbow to one who is visually impaired. To such a person the manifestations of love – which are akin to illness – would probably appear irrational, which they most likely are. Of all the guises in which love is concealed, 'love at first sight' is perhaps the most difficult to explain. To say that it is an experience in which a person feels an instant, extreme and long-lasting emotional attachment for a stranger, on encountering them for the first time, is as unhelpful as giving a clinical description of mumps or measles to someone who has never known either condition. Freud, who had an answer for everything, described 'love at first sight', in which those stricken experienced an altered world, as 'a kind of sickness and craziness, an illusion, a blindness to what the loved one is really like'.

'Love-sickness', which has been equated with mental illness, can drive a person to despair (or drink). Some of its manifestations encompass tearfulness, insomnia, loss of appetite, raised blood pressure, pain in the chest and heart, upset stomach, dizziness and confusion. The chemical serotonin, responsible for maintaining mood balance, when measured in people falling in love, was found to have dropped to levels observed in patients with Obsessive Compulsive Disorder in which a malfunction of the brain causes severe anxiety and obsessions and thoughts or images get played in the mind over and over again. While for some people love is transitory, and for others a source of despair, for many it is a life-sentence from which they are unable to escape even if they want to.

In the classical world erotic love was described as a kind of 'madness from the gods', and 'love at first sight' was explained as a sudden and immediate piercing love that lodged in the victims' deepest bones. In Freudian psychology Eros (not to be confused with libido) is the life force or 'the will to love and create life', while for Jung it represents a desire for wholeness and interconnection with another human being. From the Biblical Song of Solomon 'comfort me with apples for I am sick with love', to the outpourings of Shakespeare's lovesick Romeo, idealistic love has been synonymous with the passionate male. That it is a condition for which no cure has been found is indisputable. Pity those – male and female, young and old – who have been struck by it.

Although love is universally supposed to originate in the human heart, its aetiology is in the brain. While the English have a single word for love, the Greeks recognized several different forms.

Agape, love of humanity, is the unconditional, outgoing or selfless love that sees beneath the surface and accepts the recipient for who he or she is, regardless of his or her shortcomings. This kind of love is about sacrifice – such as giving time or money to charity – and expecting nothing in return. It is used by Christians to express the unconditional love of God for his children.

Philo is the love we give ourselves and refers to 'platonic' love which leads one to desire friendship with someone. It is a warm, committed and chosen love.

Storge is the love that parents feel for their children; the love that family members or friends – particularly 'best friends' – have for each other. It is unconditional in that it accepts flaws and faults in the other and makes that person feel secure, comfortable and safe.

Eros is that passionate, emotional and erotic love or desire that arouses romantic feelings and leads someone to say 'I love you'. This kind of love is often present at the beginning of a new relationship, but it may not last because it focuses on the 'self' rather than on the beloved.

In a healthy relationship all four types of love will be present, but the liaison may last longer if the same style of love is shared.

From the erotic poems of Publius Ovidius Naso, (a.k.a. Ovid), born into Roman society in 43 BC, to our own *Playboy* magazine, 'love' in all its guises has provided a limitless supply of inspiration for the artist. Since Cleopatra captivated Mark Anthony, Queen Victoria worshipped her beloved Albert (even after his death), the upstart Wallis Simpson seduced the Prince of Wales and film stars Elizabeth Taylor and Richard Burton acted out their turbulent fascination with each other on stage and screen, the 'love' story, which feeds into our own romantic imaginations, has never failed to entertain.

With their time-honoured tales of true love and tear-jerkers which speak to the heart, novelists and film-makers have it made. Which of us has not succumbed to the appeal of rugged Heathcliff for Catherine in *Wuthering Heights*, the love of Anna Karenina for Count Vronsky (*pace* the fact that she comes to a sticky end), the heartache of Humphrey Bogart and Ingrid Bergman acted out in *Casablanca*, the plight of Doctor Zhivago torn between two women or the ill-fated passion of Emma Bovary? In these and other tales of desire and deception, love, in its various forms, is the lubricant that oils the wheels.

'If music be the food of love play on . . .' And on and on. Nowhere has love been better served than in classical music where it has been manifest – Romeo and Juliet, Tristan und Isolde – or concealed, as in the emotional outpourings of Bach celebrating his love for his wife Anna Magdalena, in his *St Matthew Passion* or in his *Sonata in B Minor* for violin and harpsichord. Brahms's *Alto Rhapsody*, his wedding gift for Robert and Clara Schumann's daughter Julie, is said to be related to his unrequited passion for the bride, and Mahler's *Fifth Symphony*'s *Adagietto* conceals a declaration of love for Alma Schindler, as does Schumann's outpourings of affection for his wife Clara Wieck. The *Kreutzer Sonata* (Beethoven's No. 9) spawned not only a novel by Leo Tolstoy but was the inspiration for Janaček's music as well as for numerous classical ballets, paintings and novels.

Passion (often unrequited) has been the driving-force for many composers. From the string quartet to opera to the full-blown orchestra, there are so many dedications to love in the classical repertoire that it would be impossible to create a comprehensive list.

Love, in all its manifestations, is the *sine qua non* of most art forms. Without it the world would be a poorer place.

10

THE POTENT APPEAL
OF CHEAP MUSIC

Without music life would be a mistake.
– Frederich Nietzsche

Nietzsche was not thinking of Edith Piaf, Frank Sinatra or Elvis Presley. In music, as in life, it's horses for courses, and while the compositions of Haydn (who helped develop new musical forms such as the string quartet and the symphony), Mendelssohn and Brahms might, in times of trouble, soothe the savage breast, there are moments when one requires not only a comforter but a spokesperson, and we shouldn't underestimate the subtlety and artistry of the simple pop lyric. Edith Piaf, worshipped by intellectual George Steiner, with her husky voice that pierced the heart, made it clear that as far as her life was concerned she regretted nothing, while Frank Sinatra, in similar mode (and while making love to the microphone), reassured us that no matter what life had thrown at him, he had dealt with it his way. How resonant is that?

We all have feelings, but many of us are not too good either at formulating or expressing them. What better way than to click on iTunes or play a CD and let Ella Fitzgerald or Bing Crosby put words and music to our emotions? There is pleasure and pain in music that you cannot get elsewhere, and no matter how highbrow we may be by inclination, how much classical music is in our listening repertoire, there are times when Bach and Telemann do not hit the spot with the deadly accuracy of songsters such as Elvis Presley – he with the sexiest hips in history – known as 'the King'.

> Love me tender,
> Love me true,
> All my dreams fulfilled.
> For my darlin' I love you,
> And I always will.

Which of us would dare say it? Where would we find the words? As in poetry, our deepest thoughts and desires are formulated by both the sentiments, rife with unearned emotion as they may be, and the music that accompanies them. To hear him say 'one more time' in a *sotto voce* that is pure gravel to his backing group or 'touch my hand and I'm a king' as if he means it, sends shivers down the spine.

Noel Coward disliked the music of Mozart which he referred to as 'like piddling on flannel'. He confused Sibelius with Delius and was himself an unexceptional pianist.

In *Private Lives*, however, his acknowledged stage masterpiece, music plays a crucial role and bears the emotional weight of the play when the brilliant, brittle dialogue cannot carry it alone. The protagonists, Elyot Chase and Amanda Prynne – divorced from each other five years previously – find themselves in the same French hotel honeymooning with their respective new spouses, when they realize that the old bond between them is still extant. The soundtrack to their poignant new entanglement is the romantic duet 'Someday I'll Find You'. While Elyot scorns the song as a 'nasty insistent little tune', Amanda has the measure of its power: 'Extraordinary how potent cheap music is', a sentiment echoed by Coward who is well aware of the importance of the music in the drama being played out and its access to the unconscious.

It is clear from his *oeuvre* that not for a moment does Coward really think any music 'cheap' nor its potency 'extraordinary'. These beliefs are endorsed by Virginia Woolf, whose diaries record that music was a central part of her life, who wrote that 'music was nearest to truth' and who used musical technique to shift from one narrative perspective to another in order to represent the unspoken thoughts and feelings of her characters. Although she was probably thinking of Wagner and Beethoven, rather than Coward and Presley, in a famous letter of 1940 she wrote, 'I always think of my books as music before I write them.'

'Cheap' music, dismissed by some as superficial or *schlocky*, is popular music. Musically and lyrically most pop songs are about love, and their content is emotional rather than intellectual. They have instant ear appeal, melodies that are recognizable and clever orchestration that contrives to deliver maximum impact. While it is true that Coward may not be Schubert, he is not a million miles away.

For many people snatches of those tunes which have a powerful emotional force are in continual occupancy in the recesses of their minds. Elvis Presley's hugely popular repertoire goes directly to that part of the brain that remembers, without rationalizing or analysing. Listening to him has been compared to listening to the metaphysical poets of the seventeenth century. We feel that he is singing directly to us. 'It's Now or Never', 'Can't Help Falling in Love', 'I've Got a Thing About You, Baby' . . . Throughout every lyric, every note of the score, there is a tenderness that flows outwards to the subjects and inwards to the sufferer. In 1973 Presley released an album entitled *I Can Help*. Millions in emotional turmoil found that he could.

While many of us were brainwashed at school or university with the notion that popular music – together with television soaps and sitcoms – have their place, they are *not* culture. *Echt* culture, the pundits would have us believe, involves serious attempts at understanding and listening, and its payback cannot be obtained without effort. But is it worth the effort? Why should you spend solemn evenings with Shostakovich when you could be singing along with the Beatles, chilling out to rock 'n' roll or playing the guitar in a pop group, pursuits every bit as valid as more cerebral pastimes? What is it about 'high culture' that leads the pundits to dismiss such apposite lyrics as 'Just Pretend', 'Suspicious Minds' or 'The Wonder of You' as 'lowbrow' and not worth listening to?

When Vera Lynn belted out 'There'll Be Blue Birds Over the White Cliffs of Dover', 'We'll Meet Again' and 'You'll Never Know Just How Much I Miss You' to put heart into our 'boys' at a time when Germany looked as if it was getting better of the allies in 1940, were the sentiments not pertinent? Were the songs not as poignant in their time as that of Beethoven's final Piano Concerto, with its triumphant finish, written from the heart as the French army was besieging his native Vienna?

While life is not simply about enjoying oneself, many forward-thinking universities have accepted the fact that today Beowolf and Shakespeare, once firmly embedded in the curriculum, have in some cases given way to pop music, cartoons and cult movies appealing directly to the young as things we need to know about. For better or worse, education is no longer exclusively about 'high culture'. An educated man or woman is one who can appreciate the first rate in everything, and is not Richard Tauber's heartstring-tugging rendering of Franz Lehar's 'Dein ist mein ganzers Hertz' ('You Are My Heart's Delight') as worthy to be on the university syllabus – for the sheer pleasure it gives and the emotions it evokes – as Schubert's *Winterreise*?

Whether or not you think that popular music is a genuine art form, whether you consider that music that entertains can also carry intellectual and emotional meaning and that opera is not the only way to blend words and music into sublime meaning, the awarding of the 2016 Nobel Prize for Literature to Bob Dylan, hailed as an heir to Keats and the only rock musician to be admitted to the American Academy of Arts and Letters, certainly put the cat among the pigeons. When Alfred Nobel left instructions that the prize should go to the person who produces 'in the field of literature the most outstanding work in an ideal direction' and that it should be awarded 'not only to belles-lettres but to other writings which by virtue of their form and style possess literary value' was he thinking of Robert Allen Zimmerman of Hibbing,

Minnesota, cultural revolutionary and anti-war campaigner?

Those opposed to awarding the Nobel Prize to the acclaimed 'musical expeditionary' – whose inexplicable fleeting moments somehow charged the air, who considered himself a poet first and a musician second, who was the most literate and bookish pop star in history, who took his inspiration from the Bible as well as from Dickens and Thucydides – because his lyrics did not qualify as 'literature' were barking up the wrong tree. They did not understand that not all 'pop' music was equal, and while the study of it was once disdained as a 'second-rate discipline for third-rate academics', the Nobel committee credited Dylan with having 'created new poetic expressions within the great American song tradition'.

Whether you think popular music cheap or not, whether you consider it good or bad, whether you like punk rock, folk, traditional ballads or the classical repertoire, music is a matter of personal choice and should remain so.

11

BÊTES NOIRES
AND CLICHÉS

Bête noire: 'A person or thing that one
particularly dislikes'

Cliché: 'A phrase or opinion that is overused
and betrays a lack of original thought'
– *Oxford English Dictionary*

'Bête Noire', literally 'black beast' in French, means someone or
something one instinctively dislikes and tries to avoid, a thorn
in one's side or an object of aversion. It usually refers to a person
with whom one is fixated and whom one regards with a mixture
of fear, hatred and fascination.

The first known use of the term 'bête noire', or nemesis, a
French axiom for which there is no satisfactory English transla-
tion, was in a letter written by Marie de Rabutin-Chantal (a.k.a.
the Marquise de Sévigné), in 1689 to a French aristocrat.
Renowned for her elegant letter-writing, Madame la Marquise
stated, 'I fear nothing so much as a man who is witty all day
long.' Such a man would be one of her several 'bêtes noires', an
expression that has no real equivalent in another language.

We all have pet hates or aversions, many of them illogical, as
well as things we cannot stand and which are regarded as 'the

bane of our lives'. They vary from people whom we dislike very much or who annoy us to doing our tax returns, having to be polite to time-wasters, politicians who make promises they don't keep, readers who turn down the page corners of a book, dilatory eaters who lay down their knives and forks after every mouthful, guests who outstay their welcome, reluctant purse-openers, menacing waiters bearing outsize peppermills, the insincere injunction to 'have a nice day', Christmas, the touch of velvet, the squeak of chalk on blackboards, fireworks and loud bangs . . . I could go on.

A 'bête noire' can refer to a person as well as an object. We all have family or friends who annoy us, people who for no reason of which we are aware evoke feelings of hostility before they even open their mouths. The very mention of their names, or their physical presence, is enough to provoke reactions of which we are frequently ashamed. While we may do our best to disguise unbidden or inappropriate feelings, we may recoil inwardly at the sight of a well-meaning neighbour, an otiose politician or a plate of rice pudding. For an explanation of these reactions we have to go back to Freud, who asked not 'how the Germans came to murder the Jews' but how 'the Jew came to attract this undying hatred'.

In many action movies, as well as in life, the hero or heroine has a personal bête noire. This can be an object, or a fact, as well as a person. For civil rights campaigner Martin Luther King it was racism, but a bête noire can be anything from bedbugs to barbecues. We are all likely to encounter people or situations that make us 'see red'. These can vary from unamusing stand-up comedians, next door's cat, shrink-wrapped packages that are impossible to open, piped music, drivers who hog the middle lane, readers who spit on their fingers before turning a page of a book . . . The list is endless.

If there is something or someone you hate more than anything else in the world, then that is your particular bête noire, not to be confused with the minuscule black insects – spiders, woodlice and cockroaches – which invade country bathrooms, kitchens and bedrooms and are known in France as *petites bêtes noires*.

Which brings me to the bête noire's close relation, the cliché, which to Flaubert 'sounded like tinnitus' and is a 'rabbit warren' of overworked phrases. The 'cliché', a trite saying that we all hate but frequently use, is a word that originated in mid-nineteenth-century France. It referred to 'a metal stereotype or electrotype block' used in printing, hence a hackneyed expression, phrase or opinion which has been used so many times that it has lost its original connotation. Anyone who speaks English knows precisely what we mean when we say that there are 'plenty of fish in the sea', that something is 'as easy as pie' or 'every dog has his day'. Phrases such as 'the elephant in the room', 'it's not rocket science,' 'hit the ground running', 'it does what it says on the tin', 'the devil is in the detail', 'grind to a halt' and 'the world is your oyster' are only the 'tip of the iceberg', while 'past its sell-by date', 'because I'm worth it', 'sing from the same hymn sheet', 'calling the kettle black', 'time will tell' and 'fit as a fiddle' add nothing to the richness of the English language.

Some clichés are literal and others figurative, some are thoughts which are true, some are stereotypes, some facts and some not true. No matter which category they fit into, if they were only to be used sparingly they would probably still be acceptable because they were originally inspired by experiences of everyday life. A cliché cannot be accepted as fact. If anyone were to take a saying such as 'it's raining cats and dogs' at face value they would never venture out in the rain. Literal clichés such as 'All's well that ends well', however, mean exactly 'what it says on the tin', and no further analysis is necessary.

Clichés sneak into the English language confirming the mundane, the expected and the banal. While to know 'the price of everything and the value of nothing' doesn't, of course, refer to us, we all know someone to whom this truism applies. Who has not been guilty of using phrases such as 'all bells and whistles', or 'all things being equal' (from the Latin *ceteris paribus*), clichés that trip lightly off the tongue? There are many things that make us angry and which we should avoid 'like the plague' (the Spanish flu endemic of 1918–19). Which of us has not had to go 'back to the drawing board' or had a 'bad hair day'?

The cliché, or hackneyed phrase, recognized as the *lingua franca* of the uneducated and the lazy, cannot, however, be summarily dismissed. We have only to look at the biblical 'jot and tittle', the ubiquitous 'bear with me' (beloved of call-centre workers) and 'at his wits' end' or to read the works of Shakespeare, Milton, Dickens and Ian Fleming – 'shaken, not stirred – to observe new (and clichéd) ways of seeing the world.

Clichés should not be confused with idioms, such as to have 'cold feet', 'the leopard cannot change its spots' and 'you can't make a silk purse out of a sow's ear', or proverbs, such as 'a bad workman always blames his tools', 'a cat has nine lives' or 'the creaking gate lasts the longest', none of which can be literally understood.

Those of us who know, in Oscar Wilde's words, 'the price of everything and the value of nothing', and who are aware of the many challenges to conventional thought posed by the bête noire and the cliché, may start our days by reading in our newspapers (or on our tablets) about the shenanigans of contemporary 'A-listers', go 'back to the drawing board' at the office, have a drink after work with 'movers and shakers', get home 'better late than never' and 'at the end of the day' put out the light but not – *pace*, Othello – 'put out the light'.

12

HANDS

Hold infinity in the palm of your hand . . .
– William Blake

Hands, unexamined sexual symbols, are often the first things a woman notices about a man, and she will react accordingly. Strong well-manicured hands on the steering-wheel of a car, caressing the keys of a piano or manipulating the bow of a violin can send erotic signals as powerful as any other physical attributes in a prospective partner.

While many iconic painters and sculptors concentrated their attentions on wide foreheads, manly chests or firm buttocks, Michelangelo Buonarotti (*The Creation of Adam*), Albrecht Dürer (*Praying Hands*), Leonardo Da Vinci (the *Mona Lisa*), Salvador Dalí (*Portrait d'une Femme Passionate*) and Claude Rodin (*Hands of Lovers*), among other artists, understood the anthropology and the social and sexual significance of the human hand – the most frequently symbolized part of the human body – and conveyed the emotion of a lover's touch with their depictions of hands, many of which will take your breath away.

'Speaking with our hands' is something we do without thinking, and hand signals can mean different things to different people in different situations and in different cultures.

Hand gestures in art may be *descriptive* – 'pointing' to elucidate a story or narrative – *symbolic* – hands used in blessing – or *rhetorical* – gestures that reflect and illuminate the emotions. The interpretation of the simple 'wave' depends on the words accompanying the action, the body language and facial expression and also, importantly, the cultural, social, geographical and historical context of the gesture.

In some Asian cultures the left hand is symbolic of 'yin' energy and the right hand of 'yang' energy; hands folded together or clasped symbolize allegiance and friendship.

Hidden hands in gloves or drapery – as depicted in art – indicate either that the artist has a problem with drawing or painting hands (with their twenty-seven bones), or humility and the showing of respect where it is due. Native Americans use hands as a way of symbolic communication and showcase their most eloquent speech via use of hand gestures, while in Buddhism, as well as in Hinduism, hand positions known as *mudras* are important in expressing transference of divine powers. Hands shown in various positions symbolize inherent energy such as in meditation, receptivity, unity and wisdom.

The hand has long been thought of as a conduit of power – transforming unseen energy into the world of form – and the Latin *manifestus* (clear or plain) encompasses the word *manus* or hand.

Rodin once said he 'always had an intense passion for the expression of the human hands', there 'are times when they succumb to destiny' and 'times when they seize the void and, moulding it as a snowball is moulded, hurl it in the face of Fate'.

While some experts claim to be able to psychoanalyse someone by examining his hand, and biometric parameters of the hand have been quoted as an index of schizophrenia, there is none so convinced of his diagnostic and predictive powers as the palm reader.

Palm-reading – also known as 'palmistry' or 'chiromancy' – which is practised worldwide, has its roots in Indian astrology and Roma fortune-telling. Its objective is to evaluate a person's character, or future, by studying the palm of the hand.

The *hort* line, which ends near the centre of the palm, is purported to indicate 'a fast thinker who reaches conclusions quickly'; a long, straight line (extending across the palm toward the little finger) indicates 'someone who finds themselves turning things over and over before coming to a decision'. If the line splits in two, the person is sensitive, able to see another's perspective and liable to change his or her opinion, while a long, curved line (running down toward the bottom corner of the palm) indicates a creative thinker who can imagine many possible outcomes or approaches to a situation.

Hands vary in temperature: they may be warm or cold, coarse or soft, moist or dry, while fingers may be thick and stubby or delicate and elongated. Their sex appeal must not be minimized, and the sight of them can be as evocative as a glimpse of female breast or manly chest. While eyes are the 'windows of the soul' or a barometer of emotions, and the mouth can suggest various character traits, hands are indicative of strength or weakness and are the most frequently symbolized part of the human body. They give blessing, are expressive and, according to Aristotle, are the 'tool of tools', suggesting strength, power and protection. Hands can indicate generosity, hospitality and stability, and they are used in gestures of greeting where they are often an indicator of a great deal more than friendship.

As with handwriting, how a person shakes hands can be a clue to their inner nature. Sweaty palms can be the sign of an anxious person whose sympathetic nervous system has become overactive. A limp handshake – which can give the impression that you are making contact with a dead fish – may indicate low self-esteem. A quick grasp, followed by a release, as if your hand is being shoved aside, suggests 'my agenda matters and yours does not'. The two-handed shake – popular with politicians – is thought to convey the meaning of warmth, friendship and trust: if his or her left hand stays on your hand, however, it is sincere, while if it creeps up your wrist, your arms or your elbow he or she is trying to get something from you. If you feel your hand being pulled towards the person or being guided in a different direction – towards a chair or a corner of the room – you are shaking hands with a control freak who wants to dominate everything (including you).

When someone grabs your fingers – rather than your hand – he or she means to keep you at a distance and may be insecure. If, in addition, that person *crushes* your fingers he or she is adding a show of personal power in order to keep you at arms' length.

The 'bone crusher' will squeeze your hand until you cringe, which is designed to intimidate you. He or she may respond positively to you if your grip is equally strong. If another person's thumb and fingers touch only the palm of your hand, he or she may fear connecting at a deep level and have difficulty in building relationships. If the hand-shaker holds his or her hand horizontally – and above yours – he or she feels superior to you. If the person extends the arm so that you can't get close, he or she needs space and is not letting you in. If you want to be that individual's friend you must give him or her the physical and emotional distance required.

Hands are an important component of sex appeal and are closely associated with touch and sensuality. There are more nerve endings in the hand than in any other part of the skin.

'Speaking with our hands' is something many people do without thinking, and hand gestures can mean different things to different people in different situations. The meaning of a simple 'wave' varies according to the speech which accompanies it, as well as the body language, the facial expression and the cultural, social, geographical and historical context of the gesture; while to the conductor of the orchestra a swishing hand gesture indicates that the strings must play louder, a similar signal from the slave-master will be interpreted as a command to increase the lashes of the whip.

The disparate roles of the right and the left hand are made manifest in the Old Testament. They play an important part in Jacob's final blessing to his grandsons, Ephraim and Manasseh, whom Joseph places at the left and right side of the patriarch, expecting his father to place his right hand on Manasseh (the first-born) and his left hand on Ephraim, in order to give them his blessing. Jacob, however, crosses his hands and places his right hand on Ephraim and his left hand on Manasseh. Despite Joseph's objections, Jacob explains his action by asserting that Ephraim will be greater than Manasseh.

According to the Old Testament, the *torah* was given with the right hand of God – representing the Attribute of Mercy – while his left hand signified the Attribute of Judgement.

The significance of hands throughout literature is illustrated by Emma Bovary's gloved 'hand' seen trailing outside the carriage window, as she presumably gets up to no good with her lover Léon; the ultimate goal of the Bennet sisters in Jane Austen's *Pride and Prejudice*, to achieve a wealthy man's 'hand' in marriage, foreshadows the fact that Elizabeth does eventually win Darcy's 'hand'.

The hand is the most frequently symbolized part of the human body. It can represent strength, power and protection as well as generosity, hospitality and stability, and the act of 'shaking hands' symbolizes both greeting and friendship.

We use our hands to demand, promise, summon, dismiss, threaten, supplicate, express aversion and fear, to question and deny: we employ them to indicate joy, sorrow, hesitation, confession and penitence, to measure, quantity, number and time. Hand gestures vary as symbols. They can bless, consecrate, transfer guilt and bestow healing. We raise them to swear honesty, love, adoration and salutation; clasp them to embrace peace, alliance and friendship; associate them with negligence, arrogance, purification, cleanliness and innocence; through our hands we can demand, promise, summon, dismiss, threaten, supplicate, express aversion or fear as well as question and deny; with them we indicate joy, sorrow, hesitation, confession and penitence. Using them we are able to excite and prohibit as well as express approval, wonder and shame.

It is little wonder that hands are said to speak.

13

SLEEP

We are such stuff as dreams are made on; and
our little life is rounded with a sleep.

– William Shakespeare

What is it with sleep? We focus a great deal on nutrition and
how the food we eat impacts on our well-being but sometimes
forget the importance of a good night's sleep. We all need
sleep: early birds and midnight-oil burners. We couldn't live
without it, and, according to Carl Jung, the importance of the
dreams we have while sleeping is to produce fantasy material
that re-establishes the psychic equilibrium. A lack of sleep is
associated with a greater risk of depression and other psychiatric conditions. It can affect our physical health, our ability
to protect ourselves against infectious diseases and is associated with increased risk of heart attack, high blood pressure,
diabetes and stroke. Everything really *is* better after a good
night's sleep, but how to achieve this – other than going for
the pharmaceutical option – is open to debate and varies from
bedtime rituals such as reading or drinking camomile tea to
making sure that the area where you sleep is dark and quiet. The
hormone melatonin, which regulates sleep, is produced in total
darkness, and the longer you stay in the dark the more melatonin the pineal gland will produce. Exposing the eyes to lots

of bright, natural light during the day can help one sleep better at night.

In Shakespeare's *Macbeth* the sleep 'motif' crops up frequently. While the three witches use sleep – or the inability to lose consciousness – as a way to curse people and haunt them, poor lily-livered Macbeth wants to murder sleep, demonstrating how losing one's innocence can also mean losing one's ability to sleep. Lady Macbeth does not get off scot-free. Having lost her peace of mind because of her complicity in Duncan's murder, she is unable to sleep and indulges in a spot of sleepwalking which she regards as 'a great perturbation in nature, to receive at once the benefits of sleep, and do the effects of watching', demonstrating how feelings of guilt can lead not only to the inability to nod off but can rob one of the ability to function. That nothing has changed on the 'raveled sleeve of care' front is confirmed by the vast quantity of sleeping pills prescribed regularly by doctors and by today's proliferation of 'sleep clinics'.

Macbeth would rather be dead than go through the torture that is sleeplessness – 'the season of all natures', and the guilt, engendered by his insomnia, leads to serious torment and, ultimately, death. Would a visit to his GP because of his inability to get a proper night's rest have saved him?

According to F. Scott Fitzgerald, 'It appears that every man's insomnia is as different from his neighbour's as are their daytime hopes and aspirations.'

While sleep is a basic human function, the inability to sleep, which is both extremely common and extremely complex, is unique for everyone. It can delight, frighten and regenerate, may lead to fatigue and cannot be shared.

Many writers and artists have attempted to explore sleep through mythology – Jacob's biblical dream of a stairway to heaven; Botticelli's Mars and Venus, a painting in which the god of war is subject to humiliation. Sleep deprivation is in common use as a method of torture, and it has been likened to a form of death.

From birth we spend one-third of our lives asleep and, while millions of sleeping pills are ingested every year, it has been shown that non-drug treatments offer the best hope for tackling insomnia. Sleep hygiene, such as relaxation therapy, stimulus control and sleep restriction (Cognitive Behaviour Therapy), as well as going to bed and getting up at the same time every day and resolving worries before bedtime, have all been shown to help.

The inability to sleep can be a symptom of physical or emotional illness as well as a syndrome in its own right. It is associated with menopause, anxiety, certain prescription medicines, stress, caffeine, drug abuse, chronic pain, illness and poor sleeping habits. What hope is there for the insomniac whose unenviable state has been depicted in literature throughout the ages? It is no laughing matter and by no means exclusively a malaise of modern life.

The narrator of Chaucer's dream poem has suffered some unspecified disappointment in love and is unable to sleep: 'Day ne nyghte / I may nat slepe wel nygh noght . . .' Wide awake, he reads a book by Ovid that finally knocks him out!

Daniel Gabriel Rossetti's *Insomnia* regards the absence of sleep as a curse in which the speaker experiences some psychic closeness to his absent lover: 'Thin are the night-skirts left behind / By daylight hours that onward creep . . .'

When the novelist Wilkie Collins gives up cigar smoking he suffers from chronic wakefulness for which the laudanum he is prescribed has its own terrible consequences.

The protagonist Ralph Roberts, in Stephen King's *Insomnia*, experiences the visions that accompany sleeplessness. Not only can he detect people's auras but can see an odd race of invisible beings ('little bald doctors') who are engaged in a cosmic struggle against the Crimson King.

Sleep has been defined as 'the resting state in which the body is not active and the mind is unconscious', and the amount of sleep you need each day varies over the course of your life: sixteen to eighteen hours for a new-born baby and seven to eight hours for an elderly person. Many gene factors and multiple environmental factors influence sleep, and the results of today's research into the difference in sleep patterns between male and female fruit flies could well help to deconstruct poet Sylvia Plath's sleepless man twitching on his pillow 'immune to pills: red, purple, blue . . .'

Getting sufficient sleep is important for our physical health. In addition to directly affecting our ability to protect ourselves from infection, sleep also relates to our well-being through nutrition. By increasing the level of the stress hormone cortisol and decreasing the level of leptin (the hormone which lets your brain know you've had enough to eat), a good night's sleep can help us to make healthier eating choices.

Facile dictu, difficule factu. 'Easier said than done', and there are many zombies staggering around for whom, no matter how many sheep they count, no matter what strategies they carry out in the way of warm baths, eyemasks, herbal drinks and relaxation exercises before going to bed, a 'good night's sleep', which helps the foster both mental and emotional resistance, is out of reach.

The subject of sleep is frequently revisited in art. Perhaps the appeal for the artist is that when one falls asleep it is every man for himself: the experience cannot be shared, and it is frequently depicted through mythology. In Giorgione's erotic *Sleeping Venus* the naked goddess, whose voluptuous curves echo those of the surrounding landscape, has her hand over her pudenda – referring to her procreative powers – and her sexuality is enhanced by her apparently deep and erotic sleep. In Lorenzo Lotto's *Sleeping Apollo* sleep takes on a different connotation: it has not only robbed Apollo of his strength and might but, to judge by the abandoned books and the instruments at his feet – belonging to the nearby cohort of cavorting, naked Muses – he appears also to have been divested of his reason. This state of affairs pre-dates the lack of rationality which has become a key issue in forensic aspects of sleep. In Piero della Francesco's *Dream of Constantine* sleep is depicted as a state where only the divine becomes revealed and the sleeper can realize higher states of consciousness. This forces the viewer to ask whether or not he or she is witnessing an event that is occurring in reality or if he or she is privy to an actual dream.

That sleep may be a reversible form of death, and death an alternative form of sleep, has always intrigued writers and artists, and as late as the nineteenth century sleep and death were equated by some physicians.

Whatever the case, we will continue to dream: which is another – Freudian – story.

14

MY GRANDMOTHER'S CHICKEN SOUP

When from a long distant past nothing subsists,
after the people are dead, after the things are
broken and scattered, still, alone, more fragile,
but with more vitality, more unsubstantial, more
persistent, more faithful, the smell and taste of
things remain poised for a long time, like souls,
ready to remind us.

– Marcel Proust

Proust's *Remembrance of Things Past* and recent psychoanalytic theory suggest that eating practices are essential to self-identity and are instrumental in defining family, class and even ethnic identity. Food and related imagery have long been part of literature. From Chaucer's *Canterbury Tales*, through Ernest Hemingway with his 'oysters with their strong taste of the sea and their faint metallic taste' to Margaret Atwood who uses food and eating disorders to address issues of gender, language and sexual politics. Food has been used in literature for inspiration, plot device and as a method of revealing character.

In *East of Eden* John Steinbeck pre-empts the day when the curative powers of chicken soup, acknowledged in the twelfth century by Maimonides – who strongly recommended it for people suffering from haemorrhoids and the early stages of leprosy – would be recognized and it would become known throughout the world as 'Jewish Penicillin'.

'And Tom brought him chicken soup until he wanted to kill him. The lore has not died out of the world, and will still find people who believe that soup will cure any hurt or illness and is no bad thing to have for a funeral either.'

On paper, chicken soup is a broth made by 'boiling chicken parts or bones in water, with various vegetables and flavourings'. This is tantamount to saying that *War and Peace* is a text concocted by sprinkling several hundred pages with a variety of printed words arranged in uniform lines and binding them together.

The saga of my grandmother's 'chicken soup' began in the early mornings while she had the kitchen to herself. Like writing, for which according to Kafka 'one can never be alone enough', silence and solitude were key ingredients. They concentrated the mind.

Grandmother's saucepan – which I still have in my attic – was gross and black and big enough to bathe a baby in, acknowledging the unwritten rule that you can never make too much chicken soup (or too many roast potatoes). Covering the bird, at least three accompanying sets of giblets – and a meat bone or two if one is no purist – with cold water, it was set on a low flame until it came to the boil when the reaction of the boiling water with the chicken produced a thick foam or 'scum' which rose swiftly to the surface and had to be gently and meticulously removed with a metal spoon. A small amount of salt, together with approximately another third of a pint of cold water, was then added and the pot watched *sans interruption* until once again the water boiled when the procedure would be repeated. This time-consuming ritual, carried out with infinite care until no further scum rose to the surface, required the patience of a saint, the skill of a surgeon and the eyes of a hawk. Failure to carry it out correctly would result not in a golden, crystal-clear broth but in a panful of muddy and opaque liquid pleasing neither to the eye nor the palate.

The 'skimming', which often took place over a span of thirty unhurried minutes, was followed by a lowering of the heat and the introduction of the vegetables and seasonings which would give the soup its distinctive flavour. The choice of vegetables was idiosyncratic, but there was a copious amount of them. My grandmother used to swear by something called 'root' – a cross between a carrot and a turnip – which I believe originated in Eastern Europe whence she came but which has, sadly, faded into oblivion. Leek, celery, carrot, turnip, parsnip, swede, tomato, parsley and courgette, cut into pieces, were some of the possibilities, every cook having her favourite selection.

With the addition of salt and white pepper and a few threads of precious saffron soaked for a while in a small quantity of boiling water– some swear by the magical powers of a sugar cube – my grandmother's preparation was complete, and the soup was left to simmer, infinitesimally gently, preferably for six to eight hours, by which time it would have transmogrified into a translucent and golden liquid which pervaded not only the kitchen but the entire house with a fragrance guaranteed to stimulate a remembrance of things past. Some three hours into the cooking time (according to the age of the bird) the chicken was removed from the broth, the meat taken from the bones – later to be disguised with a tasty sauce for the table – and the carcass returned to the saucepan.

This was by no means all. When the cooking, preferably carried out twenty-four hours before the soup was to be served, had been done and the contents of the saucepan cooled, the resulting liquid was strained into a clean bowl through a fine-meshed sieve, the by now flaccid vegetables discarded, and the giblets, for those with enough stomach to fancy them, added to the broth. When the soup had cooled, the bowl was put into the fridge where by the following day, with a bit of luck, it would have turned into a fragrant jelly and the fat would have solidified into a rich layer on the top. This *schmalz* had to be carefully removed with a slotted spoon and discarded or used for frying or baking (with no regard on the part of my grandmother, who lived to a ripe old age, for the undesirability of hydrogenated fats). Any small beads of residual fat idling on the surface were then soaked up using a clean tea-towel or, later on, kitchen paper.

The soup, while now ready, was not yet complete. The addition of matzo balls, which Jews have been eating since the eleventh century (Marilyn Monroe famously said she didn't know matzo had balls), made with matzo meal, beaten egg, chicken fat and water, rolled with wetted hands to make spheres as solid as bullets (sinkers) or ethereal as gossamer (floaters), was mandatory. This garnish was sometimes varied by the addition of 'lokshen' (vermicelli), fresh vegetables or shreds of exhausted chicken meat added while the soup was gently reheated. Once again my grandmother watched the cauldron like a hawk. If she turned her back for a moment the soup might boil and lose its translucence, never to be restored.

The chicken soup was a two-day job. Was the effort that went into the preparation of what, at the end of the day, was no more nor less than a bowl of soup worth it?

Eating is a basic human activity necessary not only for survival but which is inextricably connected with social function. Eating habits, the choice of companions and the reasons behind these choices are fundamental to fostering an understanding of human society. Dining rituals provide a framework that directly reflects and expresses human desires and behaviour.

Today, much that the heart – or the stomach – desires is pre-cooked, and I don't know if it is my imagination or if the 'ready-meals' which fill so many supermarket trolleys really taste of nothing so much as the brightly coloured box in which they are packaged.

I would not wish the 'old days' back, but I sometimes wonder whether we have locked the door on a heritage informed by culinary tradition and thrown away the key. While the French have their frogs' legs and their cassoulets, the Italians their pasta, the Germans their Tafelspitz, the Bangladeshis their rice, the Hungarians their goulash, the Pakistanis their chapattis and the Indians their sambas and rasams, will my own occasional efforts – effort being the operative word – to recreate my grandmother's chicken soup and pass the recipe on to my daughters, preserve, for a generation at least, my own past?

15

GRIEF

Now thou art gone the use of life is past,
The meaning and the glory and the pride,
There is no joyous friend to share the day,
And on the threshold no awaited shadow.

– Sappho

Grief is unique in that it cannot be conveyed, passed from one to the other of us with any hope of comprehension, any more than can the taste of a freshly roasted chicken or the pangs of childbirth. It is the multifaceted response to loss, the emotional suffering you feel when someone is taken away from you, when everything alters but nothing changes. It is the price you pay for love. 'Only people who are capable of loving strongly can also suffer great sorrow,' said Tolstoy.

The way grief affects you depends on many things, such as the nature of the loss, your upbringing, your beliefs or religion, your age, your relationship. While there are those who behave as if sadness is an inconvenience that can be avoided by rationalizing – or going for a brisk walk – they will inevitably be proved wrong.

Grief for the dead is a wound that never heals, a pain that proves we are human. Watching someone you love die slowly is just the most horrible thing. Often it is a loss so devastating that we are unable to discuss it with anyone. The only cure for grief is grief, and one of the saddest things about losing a life-partner is that with their passing you have lost not only the opportunity for physical intimacy, the feel of a warm body next to yours, but the possibility of ever being lovable again. No matter how you look at it, the idea of a world in which the loved one does not exist makes no sense. It is impossible to concede that he or she has simply *disappeared*, and while for the Greeks tragedy's power to cleanse and purify was cathartic the very idea seems absurd.

The fashion designer Yves Saint Laurent said, 'The most beautiful clothes you can dress a woman in are the arms of a man she loves.' When those encircling arms are removed a woman feels herself not only vulnerable, open to any slight, real or imagined, but worthless. The only way the death of a loved one is not meaningless is to see oneself as part of a greater whole; a family, a community, a society. If you don't, mortality is a horror: if you do, it is not. In order to feel that life is worth while one needs to seek a cause beyond oneself and not fall into the trap of experiencing the patent happiness of others – the closeness of couples, the intimacy of lovers, the comfortable silence of two people at one with each other – as an affront.

Whereas before there was too little time, now there are too many hours in the day that have to be filled. New ways must be found to learn how to exist, how to discover happiness, how to seek out fresh pathways and how to make new connections, for, no matter how much we wish it, how much we yearn, how much we cry for the beloved to come back, life will never be the same again. There is nothing we can do with suffering except suffer it. It is an existence for which one is unable to prepare and which is impossible to contemplate. It is immaterial for how long the writing has been on the wall, how slow the decline, how inevitable the downward slide, the end comes as a tsunami, and there is no one with whom to share the shock of being alone, no one with whom to do nothing, no one to protect you from being buffeted from pillar to post, no one to rescue you from being adrift in a hostile world. Where once there was a shield against the slings and arrows of daily life, now there is none: you are fair game for jibe and innuendo. In a single strike, intimacy, hitherto taken for granted, has been blown out of the window, never to return. There is no one to touch as of right, no one with whom to sit in the amicable silence of two people who love each other, no one with whom to gossip, no one to whom to share the *faits divers* from the newspapers, no one upon whom to unload anxieties, no one to whom to turn for advice or reassurance, no one with whom to ratify the good news and the bad. Every decision must be taken alone. No longer part of a couple, you find yourself adrift in the pristine acres of your bed, abandoned in a hostile world in which even shoes come in pairs. The more you were friends, the more you were lovers, the harder it is. What was turned inwards must now be turned outwards. New beginnings are hard. We suffer single-handedly. No one understands. Time is a great healer. So they say. Who are 'they'? What do they know? The only panacea is to have the loved one back, to see his face, to hear the music of his voice, to feel his touch. Where is the light at the end of the tunnel? How can there be light when the light has gone out?

There is no manual to tell us how grief must be managed. Do we hasten to the charity shop with our beloved's clothes, his jackets and ties, her sweaters and coats – holding on to just one familiar garment on the off-chance that they will return – or do we keep them as comfort blankets beside the urn which contains their ashes, in the drawer or in the wardrobe? Do we numb anyone who will listen with tales of the departed's exploits and catalogues of their virtues, or do we skirt around the subject of their demise, avoid any mention of their name?

Colin Murray Parkes in his book *Love and Loss* wrote, 'Loving and grieving are two sides of the same coin: we cannot have one without risking the other'. People are not objects. They are not interchangeable. They are not jugs or vases. 'The greatest music, like the greatest drama, is the saddest, and its greatness stems from the emergence of meaning out of discord, loss and pain.'

The pain of inner loneliness is universal. Rather than focusing on the grieving self, however, and eventually realizing that circumstances, no matter how unacceptable, cannot be altered, the bereaved must arrive at the conclusion that he or she is powerless to change anything but his or her own disposition. Bereavement is universal and part of the experience of love which, for one or the other partner, must inevitably come to an end. Ways must be found to feel longing and to conquer it, to find new meaning in life before one falls into the pit of perpetual grief which is not an attractive proposition. All beginnings are hard, and the passing of a loved one is no exception. Ecclesiastes tells us that there is 'a time to live and a time to die'. Contrary to the beliefs of those who have been left behind, death does not render their very existence worthless. Change of circumstance, no matter how seemingly cruel, is part of life, and it is useless either to deny or attempt to suppress it. More helpful is to try to channel and control the events that have taken place. Contentment springs up in the mind, and it is futile to try to change anything but one's own disposition.

No one has done grief better than C.S. Lewis following the death of his beloved wife. 'Bereavement is a universal and integral part of our experience of love. It follows marriage as normally as marriage follows courtship or as autumn follows summer. It is not a truncation of the process but one of its phases; not the interruption of the dance but the next figure.'

There is no denying that a truly happy partnership – rather than one which is idealized – is a hard act to follow. It is a challenge that must not only be faced head on but understood. The more the bereavement can assume its proper place in the context of life, the more comprehensible the grieving. While there are two parties to the trauma that death inflicts, it is the survivor who bears the brunt. Eventually we must accept the fact that the loved one – like the bus – having completed his journey must return to the depot.

16

MARRIAGE AND THE SINGLE LIFE

Marriage is a wonderful institution, but who
wants to live in an institution?

– Groucho Marx

Einstein, Socrates and Voltaire have all had their say about marriage over the centuries. Einstein was cynical: 'Men marry women with the hope they will never change. Women marry men with the hope they will change. Invariably they are both disappointed.' Socrates was sarcastic: 'By all means marry. If you get a good wife, you'll be happy. If you get a bad one, you'll become a philosopher.' And Voltaire was cutting: 'Marriage is the only adventure open to the cowardly.'

The definition of marriage varies according to different cultures, but it is principally a union of two people in which interpersonal relationships, usually sexual, are acknowledged. In some cultures marriage is considered to be compulsory before any sexual activity actually takes place.

It is widely accepted that the origin of marriage was 'to create a legal contract by which a man could acquire a female slave'. In some quarters this is only slightly less obvious today and cannot be summarily discounted. This was brought home in a contemporary play in which the opening sequence has a newlywed couple returning from formalizing their relationship. When they enter the marital home, the husband chills out on the sofa, loosens his tie and says to his bride, still in her wedding finery, 'How about a nice cup of tea?' to which her reply is 'Thank you, darling, that would be lovely.' This misunderstanding – he is suggesting that she make the tea, and she thinks that he is offering to make her a cup of tea – sums up the 'female slave' theory, which is still, in some partnerships, only marginally less pertinent.

Since the late twentieth century major social changes have taken place in Western society. Male and female roles have been significantly redefined, and many men – ostensibly – now step up to the plate. While today any (young) man worth his salt cooks and does his share of shopping and household chores, he rarely downs tools when a child is sick, helps him or her, as a matter of course, with homework, or – pleading an 'urgent meeting' – accompanies the child to the dentist's or the doctor's.

How far back does the concept of marriage – a ceremony followed by a continued monogamous relationship – go?

According to the Bible, the ancient Hebrews were polygamous. King Solomon allegedly had 700 wives and 300 concubines, and in cultures throughout the world, including China, Africa and among nineteenth-century Mormons, men have taken multiple wives. In the Muslim world polygamy still persists, and the idea of marriage as a sexually exclusive, romantic union between one man and one woman is a relatively recent development. According to historians, until two centuries ago, monogamous households were a tiny proportion of the world population found only in Western Europe and in small settlements in North America.

The first recorded evidence of marriage (contract and ceremony) dates to 4,000 years back in Mesopotamia. In the ancient world marriage served primarily as a means of preserving power, with kings and other members of the ruling class marrying off daughters to forge alliances, acquire land and produce legitimate heirs. Even among the lower classes women had little say over whom they married, and the purpose of marriage was to produce heirs, hence the Latin *matrimonium*, derived from *mater* (mother).

In ancient Rome marriage was a civil affair governed by imperial law. But in the fifth century, when the Roman empire collapsed, Christian Church courts took over and elevated marriage to a holy union until, in 1215, marriage was declared one of the Church's seven sacraments, alongside baptism and penance. It was not until the sixteenth century that the Church decreed that weddings be performed in public by a priest and before witnesses.

For most of human history love played little part in marriage which was considered too serious a matter to be based on such a tenuous emotion. In fact love and marriage were once widely regarded as incompatible, and in the second century BC a Roman politician was expelled from the Senate for kissing his wife in public – behaviour the essayist Plutarch condemned as disgraceful.

In the twelfth and thirteenth centuries European aristocracy viewed the extramarital *affaire* as the 'highest form of romance', and it was the French philosopher Montesquieu who wrote that 'any man who was in love with his wife was probably too dull to be loved by another woman'.

It was not until the seventeenth and eighteenth centuries, when Enlightenment thinkers pioneered the idea that life was about the pursuit of happiness, that marrying for love, rather than wealth or status, was advocated. This trend was augmented by the emergence of the middle class, which enabled young men to select a spouse regardless of parental approval. As people took more control of their love lives they began to demand the right to end unhappy unions, divorce became more commonplace and the institution of marriage changed dramatically.

For thousands of years law and custom had enforced the subordination of wives to husbands. But as the women's rights movement gained strength in the late nineteenth and twentieth centuries wives slowly began to insist on being regarded as equals, rather than as their husbands' property. With the rise of effective contraception, marriage was fundamentally transformed and couples could choose how many children to have, or – with the advent of the contraceptive pill in the 1960s – not to have children at all. If married couples were unhappy they could divorce, and today almost 50 per cent of couples do just that, and marriage has become primarily a personal contract between two equals seeking love and stability. This new definition has opened the floodgates to gay, lesbian and trans-gender couples who now also clamour for the right to marry.

Same-sex unions are by no means recent phenomena. Until the thirteenth century male-bonding ceremonies were common in churches across the Mediterranean. 'Spiritual brotherhoods' (same sex bonding) included the recital of marriage prayers, the joining of hands at the altar and a ceremonial kiss. While some historians believed that such alliances were merely a way to seal business deals, it was difficult to believe that these rituals did not contemplate erotic contact. It was, in fact, the sexual encounters between the men involved that later caused such partnerships to be banned and the 'marriage' ceremonies ranked with sorcery and incest.

Today married couples are in the minority and 'living together' (cohabiting without formality) and 'LAT' (living apart while committed to and in a relationship with each other) is becoming the norm. Where children are concerned, marriage – civil or religious – is still thought to be the best option. The single most important factor in a child's healthy development is the committed relationship of the parents. Long-term stability is nearly three times more likely to be found within a marriage relationship than in one where a couple merely cohabit.

According to some studies it is healthier to be married than single – although marriage guidance counsellors are kept pretty busy – and according to statistics unmarried people have a significantly higher risk of death from cancer than their married counterparts. Being single, however, through choice or circumstance, doesn't necessarily mean there is something wrong with you, and having to answer to no one but yourself can seem an attractive option. Whether this comes about by choice, by mutual consent, by failure to find a suitable partner or is imposed upon one by the death of a spouse or by divorce, it implies a freedom that many people who have opted for commitment of one sort or another do not enjoy. The upside of 'going it alone' is that you don't lay yourself open to being judged or scrutinized, there can be no devastating differences of opinion and the only expectations you have to deal with are your own. Reducing and lowering the amount of stress in your life can have significant benefits, and you are not answerable to anyone for your behaviour or your feelings. On the emotional front, there is no pressure upon you to act in a certain way, leaving you at liberty to feel what you feel. Independence, despite its inevitable bouts of loneliness, which can at times be devastating, is an attractive option free from the jealousy and possessiveness that destroys many relationships. While being single may help you to 'know' yourself and the person you really are, 'sharing' with another human develops your caring side and provides a buffer against illness and adversity. Having a husband, wife or partner who is both friend and confidant makes one feel that one is needed as well as bestowing positive feelings of comfort, security and trust upon one. Another advantage to coupledom – whether ratified or not – is having another human being with whom to enjoy both the good times and the not so good and so create new memories.

Humankind is not solitary by nature, and most of us crave companionship. Life is enhanced when experiences can be shared with a 'significant other' who has similar interests to one's own and who loves one unconditionally. With or without religion, marriage is an accepted way for couples to show commitment. While it is true that marriage often means that every decision will be a compromise, and that it entails the loss of freedom to do as one pleases without considering anyone else, there are many advantages in having a lover, friend and confidant by your side and on tap. Statistically, couples who marry have been shown to stay together longer and are more likely to bond for life. Although there may be something to be said about finding inner peace and fulfilment on your own, someone totally wrapped up in themselves makes a very small parcel.

It is the urge to procreate, however, that provides the greatest incentive to 'pledging one's troth'. While the jury is still out, the desire to provide one's children with a stable family and the very best and most secure start in life is the finest reason for tying the knot. Marriage gives a child two parents who can help him or her develop into a balanced and happy adult. With two role models he or she will have twice as much emotional and practical support.

'In sickness and in health' may be a relic of times gone by, but it is a pledge worth considering when the overwhelming advantages of marriage, or civil partnership, are taken into account.

17

THE CYBER WORLD

Every day is Christmas.
– from a song by Colbie Calliat

We live in an era in which life would come to a standstill without technology, which is advancing so fast that computers could soon solve every problem. Even the least informed of us who buys a railway ticket, makes a telephone call or opens a bank account uses this know-how indirectly. The secrets of human life are quietly being transferred to the digital brains of machines, and every second they learn more about us through the vast amounts of data we thinkingly, or unthinkingly, put online. Social networks and internet-connected services are helping machines learn fast. The internet has become an essential part of life and is the hot topic of discussion. Driverless cars and trains, deliveries by drone, robot assistants and mechanical carers – who can monitor the vulnerable, communicate with the demented, look after the elderly, dispense tea and sympathy to the lonely, supervise medication, help round the house and revolutionize the care of an ageing population – will before very long become commonplace. Looking further ahead, our children or grandchildren will live to enjoy the potential applications of microscopic transistors which will mark banknotes to make them all but impossible to forge, notify the owners when their wine-bottles have been chilled to the correct temperature and warn us when the milk is out of date.

Cyber, 'relating to, or characteristic of, the culture of information technology and virtual reality', is a prefix used in a growing number of terms to describe new things that are being made possible by the spread of computers. It is a neologism which is less than a generation old and which has spawned its own vocabulary. Cyberphobia is an irrational fear of computers. Cyberspace is the non-physical space created by computer systems. Cyberpunk is a genre of science fiction that draws heavily on the ideas of computer science.

In the same category we have cyberforensics, cyberveillance, cyberbullying and cyberculture In other words, what our computers are telling us is that anything we can do they can do better.

The majority of us take the internet for granted, as an integral part of our existence. We have managed to convince ourselves that without technology life would come to a standstill and the proliferation of computers, laptops, tablets and androids and so on is – as the nineteenth-century-author Samuel Butler predicted – turning us into slaves. While there are still those who eschew technology and its relevance in life, they use it unknowingly, as virtually every industry relies on computer programs for better coordination worldwide.

Seen from a distance, the 'cyber world' resembles a twinkling star, but, according to the pundits, technology is as burning and dangerous as the sun and a trap for human beings. The more benefits it gives, the more harm it does, as we overlook its ill effects in terms of our health and emotions. Like it or not, 'cyber' or 'virtual reality' has given a new dimension to the human race. We live in a world of networking where, be it in business or social activities, the farthest reaches of the globe are never more than a few 'clicks' away and it is possible for anybody, at any time, to interact with anyone in the farthest-flung corners of the world. Businessmen promote their brands from their chairs and increase their sales without leaving their desks. Book-lovers with Kindles or other electronic devices have access to volumes without adding clutter to their shelves. Video interactions, such as Skype, help keep families together, game zones (frequently abused in the eyes of parents) keep the children entertained, and information spreads faster than newsprint. The cyber world provides instant answers for students and disseminates wisdom to the inquisitive child.

While the universe has shrunk, populations carry a world of knowledge around in their pockets, human beings forget the importance of family and friends, and for many youngsters, hard-wired to the internet, physical activity is sacrificed, leaving them at risk for lifestyle disorders.

Cybershopping is one of the phenomena which have opened the doors of growers, producers, manufacturers and retailers to the savvy, the lazy and the housebound to whose doorsteps the virtual cyber world delivers bounty from the bread baskets of the real world.

While the UK's online grocery market – valued at £9.57 billion a year – is the second largest, after that of China, online shopping, a key growth sector, has the highest e-commerce penetration in Europe. Whether it is haute couture, T-shirts from Sri Lanka, plants for the garden, tickets for the opera, Open

University courses, takeaway meals or toothbrushes, cyber-shopping is responsible for the battalions of couriers and the proliferation of parcels and pollution. For the techniconsumer the internet is king.

Without leaving the house or workplace – although you are not strictly allowed to shop online in your boss's time – you can furnish your house, plan a holiday, enter a competition, research a novel, get the lowdown on a competitor or follow an abs-tightening regime, but for women nothing beats a trawl through the latest offerings of the fashion retailers with their triumphs of hope over adversity. From spotting the very top (or bottom or cover-up or accessory or undergarment) from the latest on offer; clicking on your size (if it's not out of stock) and preferred colour (likewise); to inspecting the contents of your 'virtual basket'; to selecting your delivery method (three to five days, next day or 'timed') and approving the 'add-ons', to filling in your address, followed by your designated password (which must contain at least one number and one symbol) and divulging the 'long number on your credit card', followed by the start and expiry dates, and finally the last three digits on the back of the card – and pressed the 'finish' button – there is satisfaction to be had in completing the exercise. As you reach the end of what is a cybermarathon and triumphantly click 'submit', you feel as much pleasure as if you have sat and passed a particularly tricky examination.

As you wait for the courier with your parcel, if you haven't forgotten what you've ordered by the time it arrives, and signed the electronic receipt with the electronic pen that renders your name illegible, your expectations have reached fever point. It's a pity that it's well nigh impossible to open the package without resort to your sharpest knife – which renders it unusable in the kitchen. You then extract the contents and check that it is the correct size, colour and so on, while a session in front of the looking-glass will alert you immediately (or not) as to the necessity to send back whatever it is that's arrived. This will entail completing a form, advising the sender whether you require an exchange (if so details, please) or a refund and a statement of your reasons for returning the items from a numbered list from one to ten (none of which quite fits the bill), after which exertions the wind will have gone out of your sails and you will no longer be such a happy bunny.

The attaching of the requisite labels and a trip to the post office, where the post-mistress will give you an understanding look from behind her grille, as she stamps the umpteenth returned parcel that week, plus a renewed wait for what you hope will turn out to be an 'exchange' of the correct size and colour, has taken some of the gilt off the gingerbread of your virtual acquisition. But at least, you tell yourself smugly, you will not have had to put on your best bib and tucker, taken the bus or got your car out and made the effort of venturing into the shopping mall.

Online shopping is now second nature. Where did it start? The first known internet purchase was in 1994 when a pepperoni pizza with mushrooms and extra cheese was ordered from Pizza Hut. A year on Amazon sold its first book. Two decades later global e-commerce sales were calculated at upwards of $1.2 million, and e-commerce, the online juggernaut, had taken off.

If there are dangers lurking – one of the gravest being the threat of your credit card and identity being appropriated through the online purchase procedure – they are hidden, and the systems that have been put in place to combat this are remarkably efficient. Cyberfraud, however, has become a pandemic, and hoaxes occurring on the internet are simply variations of the old-style mail- or telephone-order scam: the same wine but in a new and much improved and consumer-friendly bottle. The 'cybercriminal' – usually a male between eighteen and twenty-five –is often a hacker with something to prove or a bored computer programmer who doesn't think he will get caught, and who wants to see how much he can get away with. Credit cards, or credit card numbers, are misappropriated in ingenious ways, and the tricksters do not consider themselves thieves: they are merely shining the light of truth 'on the system'. Frequently they leave tracks.

One of the fraudster's favourite tricks is to claim 'bogus' returns from a supplier. He maintains that he has sent the merchandise back, but, of course, it never arrives. He may also return a single garment but swears that the parcel contained several items for all of which he demands a refund.

Buying online is always risky. This risk doubles when shopping for clothes, since the images that untried and untested suppliers post can be misleading. The mantra is to stick to reputable sites and the ones that you know. While most websites are safeguarded, it pays to be ultra careful as to how much information you give away and to whom. The internet knows all about you anyway; if they didn't, how would they manage to advertise the very thing you are searching for every time you go online? How, otherwise, would they plug the venue and accommodation you had been thinking of exploring before you had even considered your travel plans? The geeks who run these joints and write these programs are cleverer than you. You might as well go with the flow.

The year I was born, in one of the coldest winters in living memory, saw the New York Stock Exchange crash and the beginning of a worldwide financial depression. Had you mentioned the fact that in my lifetime you could shop for food, buy your house, run your business, maintain a social network, have access to the latest research, talk to, and see, friends and relatives on the far side of the world, walk on the moon, do your shopping, control your lighting and heating, diagnose and treat your ailments and contemplate the future of driverless cars, through the internet, you would have been looked at askance. We live in stirring times. Looking ahead it is tempting to contemplate if the 'progress' we have made will be exponential, and whether the future – if we haven't killed each other off by then – will turn out to be equally exciting. The writer lives in his or her imagination.

When the digital diet becomes the only diet will the imagination prevail?

18

WIDOWHOOD

Like the sound of a distant city – the magnificent
noise of our life together – laughter, music, silence.
– Julie O'Callaghan

One of the saddest things about losing a partner is the feeling
that with his or her passing you have lost all possibility of being
desired again. As Gabriel Oak says in Hardy's *Far from the
Madding Crowd*, 'When you look up, there I shall be – and
whenever I look up, there will be you.' One day you are the love
of someone's life, nurtured and cherished, and the next you are
a 'widow', a rattling stone, a plank of driftwood. How hard is
that? What price pity? People are well meaning in their efforts
to console you. They attempt the impossible. There is no magic
cure other than to have the loved one back. You may as well bay
at the moon. We knew all along it was 'till death do us part'.
Who believes that? Who gave them the right? You float, adrift,
on a sea of well-meaning family, of relatives, of friends with
room at their tables and generosity in their hearts. How hollow
their words; how worthless their gifts. Back in your life, your
footsteps echo among the memorabilia as you turn, unseeingly,
the pages of your books, the translucent leaves of your albums.
You thought it would be for ever. This desk. That chair. His hair-
brush. Your search for lost time. The 'widows' in their protective

gaggles smile and laugh. What use their panaceas, their pity? Stamp your foot as much as you like; he will not come back.

'You'll get used to it.' The silent days; the cold nights; the ready meals; the unintended snubs. Give it time. Swallow hard. Accept their advice. Their pity. Say goodbye to the one you have lost. As if there is some great Lost Property Office in the sky! There were times when, secretively, you longed to be alone, autonomous. Now you are. 'Alone' is not synonymous with 'lonely'. You liked your own company. Not now. It is not Elysian. How dare they hold hands . . . Without thought. The touch of warm flesh. The coupledom. The walking-stick you use, now that there is no longer a supportive arm, is no consolation. Does it gossip with intimate abandon? Laugh at the same jokes. Share the same secrets. Impart the same plans. Unfurl blueprints for the future. You talk silently to yourself. Feed the squirrels. Avoid young lovers. Invisible. Wait for the willows to reach down into the water where the ducks glide gracefully; in couples.

The days are endless. You yearn for the night. The cold bed. The sweet oblivion. Things don't 'happen'. It's up to you. To make them happen: make an effort to impart some meaning to the dailyness of days. And hope that they will pass. Like a bad dream. Dreams vanish. Not this one. Where there was gossip, interchange of secrets – thoughts and desires – there is stillness. A stillness so still, so profound, that it is beyond imagination. Was it all a fairytale? The love, the laughter, the companionable silences, the interchange of ideas, the battles, the reconciliations. Now it's gone, gone, gone. And you must go on. How do they do it, these ladies who lunch in covens, huddle in their kitchens, face one another across the bridge tables, take up hobbies, learn new languages, join the Open University, as if their worlds had not been torn apart? One foot in front of the other. That's what they say. As if you were in primary school. One day at a time. It is their mantra. For a bleeding heart? Leap out of the window of your sorrow and they'll catch you in the blanket of their kindness. Not yet ready to jump, you hang on to your sadness, wrap it round you like a well-worn cardigan. Hurl yourself into the abyss of another day. Wait for the spring.

'If two people love each other there can be no happy end to it.' Hemingway was right. He didn't say *why* you don't see it coming. But you don't. Not even if it was 'a long illness bravely born'. You were busy. Too busy inhabiting an unfamiliar world of oxygen cylinders, of doctors, of district nurses, of pills and pillows, of recliner/risers, of over-bed tables, of commodes and wheel-chairs, of bowls and blankets, of clinical thermometers, of inhalers and oxymeters. Where once there were books, news-papers and journals there is respiration to be documented and inhalers in coded colours, drinks to be thickened lest they be inhaled and morphine – rather than life – to be measured out in coffee-spoons as heart-beats and 'fluids in' and 'fluids out' and everything else are documented. The ghost in the machine struggles for survival. Yet you still didn't see it coming. Well, you did but . . . You were too busy. Organizing the cavalcade, the panoply of angel faces with angel hands who flitted in and out and brought comfort of a special kind, and all you could do was watch and kid yourself it was all going to end in . . . That this 'hospice at home', with its wedge-shaped pillows and *mise en scène* of mechanical bed, which could do everything but dance, was nothing but a bad dream, a nightmare that had somehow conspired to take over your once ordered rooms, your ordered life. And despite all these manifestations of mortality, these quality-of-life invaders which had usurped your space, you still did not get it. There were still two of you. You were still a couple. Still Mr and Mrs. Still Mother and Father. Although one of you was preparing for the last of what had been so many exotic journeys, this time to a place for which there was no passport, no ticket, no standing in line for a visa. Your head was still stuck firmly in the sands of normality as your world – not so very long ago your oyster – contracted, became defined by sick-room walls. Then it is over. Suddenly. Surrounded by your extended family. 'You're so lucky!' You'd swap them all. For the cold grey body in the warm white bed. You *hadn't* seen it coming. None so blind as those who do not wish . . . You had not wished. Widowhood, with its nightmare implications, had been thrust upon you. It wasn't sudden. But it was. Hope had played its part. Until it was dashed by the reality of . . . What? Prayers in which you did not believe. And funerals. Ashes to ashes . . . It was cold in the cemetery. The earth, clod after clod, hard. You didn't want to leave him there. Not after so long. You'd thought it would go on for ever. You hadn't thought. That like a puff of smoke the past would evaporate or that the DVD of your life together would come to an abrupt stop.

You had always treasured time alone. Time for reflection, for thought. For inner life. For space . . . There is a difference. Between loneliness and longing; friendship and intimacy. With no one to hide behind, a need to socially engage after so many years of constructing a mythology, a joint memory bank, a shared database, a signalling system of grunt and touch, of troubles shared, the loneliness is fathoms deep. Finding a replacement – as if it were a car or a toaster that had given up the ghost – is not an option. Certainly not an age-mate with his personal catalogue, his baggage of infirmities. Been there; done that. It is futile to press your nose against the glass of someone else's happiness from a place that is cold and isolating. There are not, will not be, any romantic surprises. In the words of the poet Dannie Abse, 'Each day is remembrance day . . . Survival guilt endures.' There is a time to grieve and a time to stop grieving: a time to mourn and a time to stop mourning, as the widow, fabricating her 'resurgence', her return to 'normal', gets on with what is, and what has always been, life, a work in progress.

19

HAPPINESS

Two men looked out from prison bars,
One saw the mud, the other saw stars.

– Dale Carnegie

'Seek not to be Rich but Happy. The one lies in Bags, the other in content.' This seventeenth-century admonition by Quaker William Penn might not find so much resonance today when the divide between rich and poor has grown obscenely wide and seemingly unstoppable. While multimillion-pound sheiks, entrepreneurs, footballers and pop idols unashamedly lead increasingly selfish and stellar lives, the proliferation of food banks patronized by the homeless is on the increase. 'Something is rotten in the state of Denmark.'

Most of us probably don't think we need an explanation of happiness, which has been categorized as 'a mental or emotional state of well-being defined by positive or pleasant emotions'. We recognize happiness when we have it and use the term to describe a range of feelings including pride, contentment, gratitude and sensations of intense joy. Happiness consists of impressions of well-being, combined with the realization that life is meaningful and worth while. In addition to making us feel good, happiness actually impinges in unseen ways both upon our own lives and upon the lives of others. It is beneficial to our health, improves our relationships, attracts friends, makes us more productive at work, helps us cope better with stress and trauma and enables us to become more creative. Although we all know some very disagreeable and elderly 'miseries', according to the experts happiness ensures that we live longer.

Perhaps the dominant findings from happiness research is that social connections are key. Intimate relationships – including romantic liaisons – are fundamental, and we should make time for those closest to us, people in whom we can confide and who will support us when we are down. Those who pause to count the chickens of their good fortune are more optimistic and feel greater satisfaction with the cards they have been dealt.

Showing appreciation to our friends for small acts of kindness generates warm feelings in both donor and recipient, while spending time and money on others – rather than on ourselves – will light up that part of our brains concerned with pleasure and reward. Likewise, giving up, rather than harbouring, grudges will make us not only feel better but will bring us closer to others. Surprisingly, it has been found that physical exercise not only has a positive effect on our bodies – relieving anxiety and stress – but is a happiness 'booster', as is ensuring that we get adequate hours of sleep. Those who prioritize material wealth over other values and compare themselves unfavourably with those who are better off, are more likely to become hostile and anxious. The citizens of countries with more egalitarian societies, such as Switzerland, are among the most contented in the world.

While genetics plays a role in positive feelings, happiness, like tomato plants, can be cultivated, but we have only to look at the lottery winners to dispel the myth that 'money will make you happy'. Another myth is that it is necessary to be in a relationship. While it is true that supportive love contributes to feelings of well-being for those lucky enough to be in one, it does not follow that people who are on their own – either by design or circumstance – cannot be happy. Contrary to popular belief, both men and women tend to get happier with age. Elderly people are more emotionally stable and experience more positive feelings than they did in youth or middle age. For those who have weathered the slings and arrows of families or careers, or both, and have now learned how to live with 'aloneness', maturity can be the happiest and most rewarding time of their lives.

While there is no satisfactory one-size-fits-all definition of happiness – it is neither profitable nor tradable and is certainly not measured by material wealth – we recognize it when we feel it and use the term to describe positive emotions such as joy, pride, contentment and gratitude, combined with a sense that one's life is good, meaningful and worth while. Happy people have more friends, are more likely to have fulfilling relationships, be more productive at work and are less likely to become ill.

While the genetic component of happiness cannot be overlooked, positive feelings can, and should, be cultivated. This can be done by making time for our nearest and dearest, visualizing what life would be like without the assets which we have, appreciating those things which are meaningful to us, looking outwards instead of inwards and practising kindness and generosity. None of this is as easy as it sounds.

Aristotle regarded virtue as being necessary for a person to be happy and believed that without virtue all that could be attained was contentment, while Epicurus had it that 'Of all the means which wisdom acquires to ensure happiness throughout the whole of life, by far the most important is friendship.'

Philodemus, on the other hand, suggested:

> Do not fear God,
> Do not worry about death;
> What is good is easy to get, and
> What is terrible is easy to endure.

Happiness, hard to grasp, is what people seek above all else. How do you know when you have it? You can neither hold it in your hand nor measure it by material wealth. A new house, a new car, the latest technology, are status symbols and by no stretch of the imagination guarantors of a contented life. Possessions can be gained and lost, and with loss comes fear. So if it isn't 'stuff', what is it? A sense of purpose? Purpose differs. People can be happy if they have something to strive for and something to laugh about, but those who have achieved their goals and already have a sense of humour can still be unhappy.

The most important thing to realize is that there is no standard and, that to 'pursue happiness' *per se* is the surest way of missing out on it. 'Happiness' means different things to different people, and while I watch with amazement friends who find happiness on a golf course, hitting a ball across a net or in other outdoor pursuits, who hunt down and collect *objets*, who produce celestial sounds from musical instruments, who find satisfaction in tending the sick and in helping others, who conjure objects of beauty from paper and paint, who fashion artefacts from clay, garments from wool and silk, produce memorable meals from bog-standard ingredients, I can only speak for myself. I am happiest when I am writing: when I transfer words that were not there before to a screen which was hitherto blank; when I discharge the heaving silo of my mind on to a page that was hitherto empty; when I surrender to the muse who has never let me down; when I put myself in the moment, allow my fingers to perform on a keyboard every bit as responsive as that of the most finely tuned pianoforte; when I produce words as light as swansdown, as heavy as precious metal; when hours pass like minutes and minutes are consumed like seconds; when somebody – that 'other' me – has produced a morning's work, be it good or bad (daily action breeds habits), I am happy. And remain so: filling in what hours remain until the next day which will find me once again, at the same time, in the same place.

When the chips are down, being happy with who you are and what you have is a decision that has to be made consciously. People need to *choose* happiness; they need to agree that they want it, deserve it and have it. The actual resolve to be happy is the final piece of the puzzle, and this depends upon ourselves. We are responsible for our own happiness and, while it is often not easy, are as happy as we make up our minds to be. Perhaps the key lies in the popular song by Vincent Youmans and Irving Caesar sung self-consciously at children's parties, to the accompaniment of clapped hands, when I was young:

> I want to be happy,
> But I won't be happy
> Till I make you happy, too.

20

WE ARE WHAT WE EAT

The body's needs are few: it wants to be free from cold,
to banish hunger and thirst with nourishment; if we
long for anything more we are exerting ourselves to
serve our vices, not our needs.

– Seneca

We all know about Michelin-starred chef Heston Blumenthal
with his desire to reinvent the language of food, his 'molecular
gastronomy', his snail porridge and his bacon-and-egg ice-
cream. But recently a Tokyo restaurant introduced a 'soil-based'
menu – which included dirt-and-potato soup, dirt risotto with
sea bass and dirt ice-cream – while 'bug-burgers', 'cricket-bars',
mealworms (toasted in a frying-pan), cockroaches, crickets,
caterpillars and longicorn beetles have introduced the notion
of insect-eating to the USA. These creepy-crawlies, if we are to
believe the hype, contain 15 per cent more iron than spinach
and as much vitamin B12 as salmon, while yoghurt made from
carrots, tomato, parsnip or beetroot is the next big thing.

In the quest to find the newest superfood, such as seaweed
and cactus water (triggering an evaluation of your lifestyle),
buyers in the USA are looking to lesser-known and exotic varieties of fresh produce such as coffee 'fruit' (not the 'beans' which
are the seeds inside the berries) used to make the health drink
Bai, while in our own kitchens – unhealthily obsessed with

'healthy eating', food fetishism (which leaves a nasty taste) and oddball diet regimes which foster a sense of moral superiority – we are urged to construct dishes with low-carbon footprints, such as 'Tuna Sashimi Pizza with Truffle Ponzu', a questionable combination of tortilla-bread fried then put in a dehydrator, raw flying-fish roe and melted cheese seasoned with wasabi and a citrus-based Japanese sauce.

Contrary to the received wisdom that 'eating fat will make you fat', we are *not* what we eat. This is a modern incarnation of an ancient superstition such as the idea that 'if you eat a deer you will run faster'. These declarations, which withstand no scrutiny, come into the same category as the prevailing 'new wives' tale' that green tea will make you happy and alkaline diets will cure cancer. People who obsess about food and its effect upon their bodies manage to bring it into every conversation and often have few other interests. Everyone seems to be competing about what they *don't* eat, and there has been a huge rise in the popularity of gluten- and dairy-free diets, disregarding the fact that cutting out important food groups could actually make us ill. Gluten-free diets, adopted by millions of people for no good medical reason, could raise their risk of getting type 2 diabetes, while giving up 'dairy' – claiming intolerance to cow's milk – may attract attention and sympathy but puts people at risk for osteoporosis. Obviously for those who have been diagnosed with coeliac disease (about 1 per cent of the population) gluten is toxic and should be avoided, but those who eliminate it unnecessarily from their diets because it is fashionable risk missing out on nutrients present in those foods, may lose energy and feel weak.

Living in the Western world we are surrounded by a plethora of information about what is good for us and what we should eat. As we struggle to source such exotic ingredients as baobab powder, Himalayan pink salt, bee pollen and chia seeds (from the plant *Salvia Hispanica* related to mint and packed with omega-3 fatty acids), we are exhorted to emulate our cavemen ancestors who survived on a diet of meat and blood pudding; to 'reboot our bodies' (excuse me!) or 'go on a journey' with the vegans (by eschewing all animal products), with the carb-free, the 5:2 practitioners, the Atkins and Dukan proponants, the raw-foodists, the vegetarians, the pescatarians, the flexitarians, the Pegans (who avoid all processed food), the Sirtists – lovers of turmeric and advocates of 'green' juice (three times a day); or slavishly follow the diktats of a variety of 'life-changing' diet gurus who exhort us to eschew regimens that carpet-bomb our blood sugar and to familiarize ourselves with the health-giving properties of every ingredient.

We who were brought up on wartime rations – when oranges, bananas, cream and avocado pears were twinkles in the food purveyors' eyes, when vegetables meant cabbage grown on our allotments, when beans (which came from the iconic tin) were baked and cheese was 'cheddar', must now learn not only eat 'mindfully' (that is, fast two days a week), source 'free-from' groceries and get our heads round such delicacies as bottarga tostada, rock samphire, fava, gum mastic, labneh, freekeh, mung beans, zhoug, za'atar and yakitori monkfish, if we are not too busy shoring up the coconut industry by sourcing and buying coconut butter and coconut oil (apparently not the same thing, although they look identical), coconut yoghurt, coconut milk and coconut flour or agonizing between two varieties of pumpkin seed.

While 'eating disorders' are rife, the 'clean eating movement' has reached fever pitch, and we are surrounded by 'wellness' evangelism, which harms as many as it heals, and those of us able to afford them are coerced into regimes of vegetable smoothies, goji berries, 'almond milk' and 'chickpea water' (a sensation in New York), 'kale' ice lollies – to make us happy – and alkaline diets to 'cure' cancer.

As food banks struggle to fight hunger, reduce waste and help the environment, the paleo or 'caveman' diet – supposedly enjoyed by hunter-gatherers whose life expectation was nearer twenty than forty – is the new weight-watching obsession of 'celebrities' (egg-white omelettes are so yesterday) and feeds into our national fixation on the flora in our stomachs, which survived very well on our erstwhile meat and two veg. Nothing, it seems, can stop the march of 'yuzu pao sauce', alfalfa sprouts, flaxseed oil, hemp, maca, protein powders and quinoa (*kinwa* to the cognoscenti), which cater to the needs of an increasing number of people concerned with 'on-the-go' nutrition. While the aim is to stay fit, little attention is paid to the fact that a regime eschewing all grains and legumes could leave people not only deficient in essential vitamins and dietary fibre but seriously constipated.

The old adage that 'what comes out of the mouth is more important that what goes into it' has apparently gone by the board, as friends and acquaintances are convinced that eating what once were 'everyday foods' is fraught with danger. These clean-eating wellness bloggers recoil, as if they were about to be poisoned, at the sight of a knob of butter on a baked potato or a swirl of cream in their soup and shudder at an innocent slice of bread, even if it claims to be 'artisan' and has never been near Chorleywood. Diets are not only annoying but are potentially dangerous. The impoverishment of gut flora is likely to be linked to obesity, and beneath the obsession for gluten- and dairy-free ingredients there can be excessive harm caused to health by excessive hygiene. Give us food that is easy to cook and which tastes good and leave the 'foodyism' to the fetishists.

While *Masterchef* contestants obsess about the 'placement' of puréed dots on their votive 'plates of food', orthorexia (an obsession with healthy eating) has taken over from 'anorexia' and a new eating disorder has arrived. Our interest in what we eat has gone from enthusiastic to neurotic. Today's trendy cooks – with their 'island' kitchens, their 'fusion' taps that dispense instant boiling water (whatever happened to the kettle?), their 'spiralizers' which turn carrots and courgettes into noodles, their salads of 'shaved' cauliflower and 'charred' broccoli, their wheatgrass and their wild rice, their sprouting seeds and edamame beans washed down with 'rooibos' tea – which claims to cure anything from headache to hypertension – are the new nutrition *mavens*, and not a day goes by when food, or some aspect of it, does not make the news.

Try as we might to buy into the image of 'natural' and 'freshly baked', we turn a blind eye to the fact that, while they may have started out in good faith, 'health' drinks are now produced under industrial umbrellas; 'chocolate' comes not direct from a cocoa plantation but from a factory and the two 'nice guys' ice-cream is no longer produced in a domestic kitchen but in the industrial premises of a manufacturing giant. The old adage not to buy or eat anything your great-grandmother wouldn't recognize as food is a pretty reliable guide.

While neologisms such as 'starters', 'mains' and 'sharing plates' have become the *lingua franca* of the restaurants where we go not to dine but to 'eat out', the aspirational middle-class ritual and social torment of the 'dinner party' has thankfully faded into oblivion. With its statutory three courses (often encompassing such show-stoppers as *Oeufs Mimosa* and *Salmon en Croute* followed by a choice of at least three home-made desserts), invitees who had to commit at least a month in advance and 'seating-plans', it has, thankfully, pretty much died the death. It has been usurped by the ubiquitous 'food to go', and the well- thumbed Cordon Bleu and Elizabeth David paperback bibles of the 1980s, their detached pages spattered with custard and gravy, have now been replaced by the glossy door-stoppers written (or dictated) by television cooks who never have to fetch their own mixing-bowls or do the washing-up. Despite the fact that 2 billion people (over 30 per cent of the world's population) suffer from malnutrition, interest in the latest food trends has never been greater.

The current spate of recipe books, their shiny covers bedizened with images of photogenic author-chefs in their photogenic kitchens, framed against Tuscan landscapes or rustic bread ovens, peddle not so much their 'signature dishes' as hefty helpings of 'gastro-porn'. Neither well-thumbed nor food-spattered from frequent usage (the more cookery books you buy the less you cook), their technicoloured offerings, predicating such ingredients as Qnola (a granola that is 25 per cent quinoa) and 'fermented cabbage' rank with mutating bacteria – the ultimate condiment for health – are destined either to end up on the coffee-table or on eBay as we backslide shamefacedly to the takeaway or consult Google for recipes, which renders these culinary bibles obsolete. Our interest in food has gone from enthusiastic to obsessive as, in the twenty-first century, we look to it to cure all ailments.

Like the Cretans, most cooks are liars. Although Jamie Oliver's *Thirty-Minute Meals* spent several weeks on the best-seller list, some of his recipes, such as 'Thai red prawn curry with jasmine rice, cucumber salad and papaya platter', took more than an hour to cook and nearly as long to clear up; while in the first *River Café Cook Book* by Rosie Gray and Ruth Rogers the recipe for Chocolate Nemesis – a dark, flourless gâteau baked in a bain-marie – resulted in a river of chocolate sauce, rather than a cake.

Today, television cookery programmes have become an addictive form of entertainment on a par with *I'm a Celebrity ... Get Me Out of Here* and *Strictly Come Dancing*, and any mention of an innovative ingredient or 'must-have' frying-pan will guarantee an overnight cull of these indispensable items from the supermarket shelves.

Despite all the stylish representations of food, the glossy cookbooks, the recipes and restaurant reviews in newspapers and magazines, despite the many esoteric and exotic ingredients on offer in the shops, despite the fact that the alpha male in the kitchen is no longer an anomaly compared with fifty years ago, people today are disinclined to cook. If you really hanker after 'butterflied sardines' or 'smoked eel covered with a snow of frozen foie gras' you will nip out to the latest fashionable restaurant or trendy eatery.

I can hardly believe how things have changed, and had I not kept meticulous records of my own erstwhile dinner parties in a 'hostess book' I would not credit it – while I am unable to justify the expense, time or energy I once devoted to these marathons.

Did I really need two chickens, one home-pickled tongue, twelve stuffed eggs, a mountain of 'golden rice', ratatouille ('very popular') and a green salad to feed eight friends? Did I really spend a week shopping and cooking to produce Consomée en Gelée and Câneton aux Cerises followed by Strawberries Cardinal and Lemon Sorbet for a Sunday-night supper? As I slaved over cold Madrilène ('fair'), Coq au Vin ('croutons hard, try pastry crescents next time') and Crêpes Pralinés avec Kissell, what on earth did I think I was I doing? When I recall the home-made taramasalata, long before it was available in tubs in every delicatessen, the time-consuming Vitello Tonnato ('very popular'), the Beef Olives Provençal, the Purée Léontine (sorry?), the pears in red wine and the chocolate/chestnut cake served on the 'best' china, illuminated by tapering candles and washed down with *mis en château* wines (affordable in those days), I remember not only ending up a nervous wreck but too exhausted to talk to my guests who, in the fullness of time, were expected to reciprocate. Where, with my large family, my large dog, two home-based jobs and many other commitments, did I get the energy? Whom was I trying to impress? While it is sadly true that many of the *dramatis personae* in my two bulging 'hostess books' have now departed this world, I did not kill them. I cemented friendships, repaid favours, did what was expected of me and lived to rejoice in the guilt-free ready meals, the home deliveries, the takeaways, the 'not-fine' dining and the convivial kitchen suppers of today.

21

FAMILIES

Happy families are all alike; every family is
unhappy in its own way.

– Leo Tolstoy

With this statement, Leo Tolstoy begins his novel *Anna Karenina*,
which is about the struggle of families to find happiness. To be
happy, the author suggests, a family must work out a number
of problems such as how to deal with money, how to deal with
children, how to divide up the responsibilities in the home, how
to manage the pressures of work, how to cope with adultery. If
a family fails to resolve any one of the difficulties they are likely
to encounter it will, by the author's definition, be unhappy. By
Tolstoy's reckoning, the only way a family becomes happy is by
confronting crises one at a time. Failure to deal with any one of
them will provoke others, and the family will not be happy. Had
he been alive today to see the transformation of what is understood by 'family' he may not have been so forthright.

The 'ideal' family not only provides its members with a
strong support system but presents society with a structure for
passing on cultural values from one generation to the next. It is
universally acknowledged that the single most important factor
in a child's healthy development is the stable and healthy relationship of the parents. That long-term stability is nearly three

times more likely to be found within a married relationship than in one in which a couple merely cohabit. Twenty-first-century families come in all shapes and sizes. Apart from the traditional 'couple' we have the single mother or father, more than one family living together under the same roof and gay, lesbian and trans-gender parents. What is understood today by 'family' includes siblings and parents (of whatever combination), as well as relatives – cousins, aunts, uncles, grandparents and step-parents – even if one does not interact with them on a daily basis. With family breakdown at an unprecedented level, having healthy relationships with family members is both important and difficult, but, no matter what type of family we have, there are going to be highs and lows, good times and bad.

With the nuclear family no longer the norm, we see more and more single mothers (and less often single fathers), two women – living as cohabitees or united by 'marriage' – with donor babies or two men making use of surrogate mothers to provide them with offspring. Parenthood – a man and a women with biological offspring – is no longer a given, and many people, either single or in a relationship, make an informed choice *not* to reproduce. Having children is not compulsory, and many adults lead satisfying and fulfilled (some would say 'selfish') lives without feeling the need to procreate. They may prefer to adopt or foster children rather than bring additional human beings – who will have an impact on the environment and consume more resources – into a seriously over-populated world. There are often valid personal reasons for choosing either to limit the size of families or to have no children at all.

This decision enables women, who still bear the brunt of child-rearing, to have a life outside the home and to compete with men in the workplace on an equal footing, even if they have not as yet achieved equal pay. Bringing up children is exhausting and expensive. Having a smaller family provides a better quality of life, more money and more time for social life, personal interests, careers and relaxation. For the childless life is simpler. The decision *not* to procreate allows women to keep working, gives them more personal 'space' and makes it simpler for them to preserve a sense of 'self'.

If the family is small it is easier to be a 'good' parent. With more time and money one is able to give a child (or children) a better education, meet their material needs and offer them a good start in life. In addition one may have better relationships with them and be less prone to worry. With a limited family, going on visits, trips and holidays, as well as including the kids in adult activities, is easier. Children in these families often tend to do better both in school and in life; there is less sibling rivalry and more opportunity for them to develop independent and rounded personalities. Such children are more likely to benefit from meeting children from other families and being involved in adult activities. They are often more self-sufficient, mature and well-behaved, and it has been shown that in later life the 'only' child can perform equally well as a child from a larger family.

According to Nietzsche, 'it is not a lack of love but a lack of friendship that makes unhappy marriages'. Having a healthy relationship with your partner and your family is important, but no matter what type of family you have, there are going to be highs and lows, good times and bad. Sitting round a table with other family members is not only good news for the waistline but means more conversation and bonding time. Children who enjoy even just occasional family meals are less prone to anxiety and more likely to enjoy raised self-esteem. Food and conversation go well together and not only promote positive feelings but enable the generations to bond, to exchange views and to learn from one another. Family meals means less time in front of the television – which encourages children and adults to eat more and to eat mindlessly – and more human interaction and bonding time which satisfies more than the appetite. Eating together encourages the release of oxytocin (the 'happy' chemical or 'love hormone'), and this boosts positive feelings, the source of numerous benefits to a better and more successful life.

Families often become blocked in their relationships by hurt, anger, mistrust and confusion. These situations are normal, and few families do not have at least some experience of them. The worst time is often during or preceding a divorce when children have to listen to their parents arguing and have no opportunity to tell them how it makes them feel or be reassured that they are not responsible for the break-up. By talking to children and confiding in them, parents may be able to explain what is actually going on.

By making a few simple changes in the way we look at the world and the way we deal with others, it is possible to create happier and more stable units of mutual caring and support. Families can be lifelong sources of strength, and it is never too late to begin the process of improving relationships – even if they are already of good quality – by developing simple strategies to resolve issues which, at first sight, may seem impossible to handle. Communication is the key to resolving conflict.

While in large families it may seem that siblings are constantly irritating one another or bossing each other around, they are also there for mutual support. If family members communicate freely and value boundaries, trust and respect will ensue.

Certain social scientists have advocated the abolition of the family altogether. The philosopher Socrates was of the opinion that a 'just' city was one in which citizens had no family ties, which the anthropologist Margaret Mead countered by regarding the family as the main safeguard to continuing human progress.

While some people still extol the virtues of family life, others believe it to be overrated because so many individuals suffer within what can be a claustrophobic relationship. Family members often don't speak to one another, and some spend years – and fortunes – on therapists, trying to undo the harm done to them by their relatives. This should not be surprising because, although we are able to choose our friends, we have no say in the matter when it comes to our relations.

Religious issues are often a cause of conflict, especially when adolescents begin to question (or belittle) their parents' beliefs and practices. A son or daughter who has had a religious upbringing may convert to an alternative faith (or none), which may well worry and concern their parents.

Family members may also have different views on social behaviour, moral matters, jobs and careers. Parents may disagree with grandparents on the way to raise their children, and sending their offspring to faith schools can also cause conflict. While Christianity and Judaism expect children to 'honour their father and mother', Islam teaches that no child should do harm to their parents – and vice versa – and Muslims are called upon to obey their parents and accept their authority even in adulthood.

While inter-faith marriages have now almost become the norm, resistance to this practice can constitute a form of self-segregation. In Judaism this remains a highly controversial issue. Orthodox Judaism refuses to accept any validity or legitimacy of intermarriage and tries to avoid assisting such marriages to take place. According to Hinduism, marriage must happen among two individuals of the same 'Varna', or caste, which can only be acquired by birth.

These variations on family life, customs and expectations lend validity to Tolstoy's apposite and often quoted pronouncement with which, more than a hundred years ago, he kick-started one of his best-loved novels. Although some cultural variations exist, and there have been many exponential changes in society, the primary role of the family is still to foster an environment in which children learn skills, morals and values and to create structure and stability in the lives of its members. When the chips are down, *Amore Solum Opus Est*: love (and family) is what it is all about.

22

ENVY AND JEALOUSY

Jealousy is both reasonable and belongs to
reasonable men, while envy is base and belongs to
the base, for the one makes himself get good things
by jealousy, while the other does not allow his
neighbour to have them through envy.

– Aristotle

Envy is the feeling of resentment or discontent at another's
position or success; to 'bear a grudge' towards someone through
coveting what that person *has*, or his or her situation, without
any ill will towards that person. Jealousy is the uneasiness that
arises due to suspicion, resentment or fear of rivalry, especially
in regard to matters of the heart. It is the emotion felt when one
thinks one may be replaced in the affection of someone or
when one fears that what one has will be taken from one. Both
envy and jealousy are powerful emotions and are nowhere
better illustrated than in the Bible.

The Old Testament's account of sisters Rachel and Leah,
cousins of the patriarch Jacob, comprises both envy *and* jealousy in what was perhaps one of the earliest-known dysfunc-
tional families. Jacob asks his uncle Laban for Rachel's hand
in marriage. He volunteers to work seven years in return for
taking her as his bride. Laban agrees but deceives Jacob by

secretly giving him a heavily disguised Leah, her older and less attractive sister. He then volunteers to give him Rachel also but only after his nephew has done seven more years of hard slog, during which time we are told that the impatient Jacob not only lay with Rachel but that he loved her more than he did her sister. It is hardly surprising that Leah becomes extremely jealous of her more attractive sibling or, that pressurized by the bigamous relationship, Rachel's true character begins to surface. When Leah gives birth to a quiverful of babies in quick succession, insult is added to injury and Rachel becomes envious, selfish, peevish, fretful and demanding. She shouts at Jacob to 'give me children or else I die', to which, losing his cool, her angry spouse replies, 'Am I in the place of God, who has withheld from you the fruit of the womb?' When Rachel finally does conceive, the birth of her second child costs her life.

If romantic love could be drummed up on demand, the 'tangled webs' we get ourselves embroiled in would no longer be woven and the world might be a simpler place. How galling must it have been for Leah, who had to have been not only *envious* of her more attractive sister but insanely *jealous* of her husband's love for her. The fact that Rachel turns out to be both a liar and a thief – deceiving both her father and her husband – doesn't make Leah feel any better. No matter how many children she bears Jacob, her husband's ill-disguised passion and preference for her younger sister haunts her for life.

An earlier biblical illustration of sibling rivalry is played out in Cain's acute *envy* of his brother Abel, which goes beyond reasonable behaviour and ultimately leads to fratricide.

Cain, a farmer, offers God a portion of his crops as a sacrifice, only to learn that God was better pleased when his herdsman brother Abel presented Him with the fattest portion of his flocks. Unable to tolerate the fact that Abel had won the Lord's favour through his offering – while his own had been rejected – Cain's insane jealousy gets the better of him, leading him to destroy all bonds of family affection and ultimately to take his brother's life.

The gift of beauty, the idea of which relies heavily on socially accepted standards, accounts for many manifestations of envy. Although the classical story of Medusa, the woman with the head of snakes, is mythical, it illustrates the effects of the powerful feelings aroused by coveting another's possessions, in this case looks.

As a human being, Medusa was a woman of such exquisiteness that a god fell in love with her and made her break her vow of chastity. Enraged, the goddess Athena (whom Medusa served as a priestess) cursed Medusa and transformed her hair into snakes, whereupon whoever gazed into her eyes would turn to stone. How envious was that? And how similar to Athena's feelings towards her protégée is the envy of today's readers of glossy magazines of the flawless cover images of airbrushed 'celebs'.

While envy is what consumes you when you covet a possession or attribute that someone else possesses, jealousy is when you fear that you may be replaced in the affections of one whom you love or desire. A well-known plot device in Hollywood movies is the 'MacGuffin', Alfred Hitchcock's term for 'that which the hero or heroine wants (envies)', in most cases a person or object of interest, such as a cache of jewels or a briefcase stashed with money. Hitchcock's devotion to the concept explains much of his success as a film director. Even if the desired object is itself obscure, it drives the story forward and is of vital important to both the goodies and the baddies. In *The Maltese Falcon* private eye Sam Spade (played by Humphrey Bogart) becomes embroiled in an intricate plot which revolves around a jewel-encrusted statuette (the MacGuffin), which had been given to Spanish King Charles V in 1539 by the Knights of Malta. In *The Raiders of the Lost Ark* the Mac-Guffin is the Old Testament 'Ark', the ultimate weapon wanted by the occult-obsessed Hitler, who is chased by globe-trotting archaeologist Indiana Jones.

It is no fun to suffer either envy or jealousy, and while both ways of thinking make one feel inadequate, they are godsends to a playwright such as Shakespeare, who refers to jealousy as the 'green-eyed monster' which – according to Iago – possesses Othello.

> O, beware, my lord of jealousy; It is the green-eye'd
> monster, which doth mock
> The meat it feed on. That cuckold lives in bliss,
> Who, certain of his fate, loves not his wronger:
> But O, what damned minutes tells he o'er
> Who dotes, yet doubts, suspects, yet strongly loves!

The idea that jealousy is 'green' probably predates *Othello*, but Shakespeare is our earliest reference to its colour. He probably made the comparison owing to the fact that at the time

Englishmen paired their emotions with colours, green and yellow being indicative of jealousy, while green was also a symbol of envy.

In Dostoyevsky's *House of the Dead*, a quarrel breaks out in prison between Gavrilka and Uncle Lomof over a girl. When Gavrilka boasts of receiving her favours, Lomov, 'mad with jealousy', drives an awl into his stupid and quarrelsome nephew's chest.

In our own time Homer Simpson, of the long-running cartoon series, explains the difference between jealousy and envy. 'I'm not jealous; I'm envious. Jealousy is when you worry someone will take what you have. Envy is wanting what someone else has. What I feel is envy.'

One cannot, of course, speak of envy without reference to Freud's famous (or infamous) theory of 'penis envy', which today is regarded as flawed: his anecdotal evidence was flimsy (Freud tinkered with patients' testimony to fit in with his propositions); he believed that women were morally inferior to men and that they were sexually passive and engaged in sex only when they wanted children. This line of thought was, of course, a consequence of the cultural and societal influences prevailing at the time and which contributed to an under-developed understanding of female psychosexual development. *Autres temps, autres mœurs*. In today's climate the psychiatrist's, the scholar's, the physiologist's, the neurologist's, the Father of Psychoanalysis's outdated theories, both on 'penis envy' and on women, no longer hold water.

According to the Babylonian Talmud, covetousness 'increases wisdom', and nowhere is covetousness more prevalent than among writers. Those who are 'unsuccessful' are forced to look on while their rivals receive critical acclaim or rise smugly from banqueting tables to accept one of the many prizes on offer to the literary Mafia. Watching the faces of the losers, one sees them struggling with the bitterness and disappointment of being passed over before, gritting their teeth, they assume congratulatory expressions for the benefit of the cameras.

Behind every book is a person who puts his or her time and talent into every page and who *minds* when other writers receive lucrative deals from major publishing houses for books they consider inferior to their own. Career novelists must write several books and keep them in the public eye – in print or as e-books – to earn enough money to quit the day-job. It is hardly surprising that writers are 'envious' of what is, falsely, perceived as 'overnight success'.

There is a perception that because a book doesn't sell it is not as 'good' as those that do. If it's any consolation to those authors who have been 'remaindered' or – even worse – 'pulped', there are many reasons for this ignominy. The author may have put his or her guts into a heart-wrenching account of a life-threatening illness, but, as her agent will tell her, when it comes to publication either she has missed the bandwagon and 'misery chronicles' are no longer the hot ticket or that the publisher, especially if he is a sardine in a tank full of sharks, may not (and this is the usual scenario) have been able to afford the publicity on which every book depends for success. If this is the case, few people will have heard of you, which reinforces the opinion of American comic Stubby Kaye that 'the circus doesn't creep into town'.

In his novel *The Information*, a disturbing tale of an unsuccessful writer frantic over his friend's success, best-selling author Martin Amis describes the bad choices one can make whilst beset by 'literary envy'.

Envy is one of those emotions to which no writer willingly admits, although the guru, Gore Vidal, was at least honest when he said, 'Every time a friend succeeds I die a little.'

If you are crazy enough to put your head above the parapet, if you strongly believe there is a value in literature, if you want to make writing your *schtick* you should not be surprised to find that both envy and jealousy are your bedfellows.

23

I REMEMBER IT WELL

Am I getting old? Oh, no, not you . . .
– Maurice Chevalier

Many people reading this will not remember or indeed have heard of Oscar winner Maurice Chevalier. Born in Paris in 1888, he was a café singer and popular star of French musical revues. In 1929, the year I was born and the year cinema 'talkies' came into existence, Chevalier abandoned his first job as an acrobat and broke into movies where he teamed up with co-star Jeanette McDonald who labelled him 'the quickest *derrière* pincher in Hollywood'. If anyone today remembers Chevalier – with his signature tuxedo and straw boater – it will be for the movie *Gigi* of 1958 which featured the songs 'Thank Heavens for Little Girls' (subject matter which would be deeply suspect today) and 'I Remember It Well', a romantic paeon of love to Chevalier's co-star Hermione Gingold, composed by two other 'oldies', Alan Jay Lerner and Frederick Loewe. Popular as Chevalier was in his time, people everywhere assuming a French accent and gravelly voice in an attempt to imitate him, today – a lone figure, with no backing group, no febrile timpanist, no masturbatory guitarist, no stoned pianist, no flashing strobe lights – he would be booed off the stage for unearned sentiment. So much for fame.

The year I was born saw the collapse of the New York Stock Exchange, the banishment from Russia of the Marxist revolutionary Leon Trotsky and the publication of Ernest Hemingway's *A Farewell to Arms*. It was a pre-war world of domestic servitude and unheated houses in which ice had to be scraped from the inside of the windows in winter, doorsteps had to be whitened – or cardinaled red – middle-class children were expected to be seen and not heard and autocratic fathers were waited on hand and foot by subservient dinner-on-the-table wives. 'Home', where there was one, was a rented working-class 'two-up, two-down' hovel or a middle-class net-curtained palace in suburbia in which the husband and father 'who must be obeyed' was King. It was a strange life in which my behatted mother, the ubiquitous shopping basket over her arm, ventured forth daily for the next meal at an old-fashioned Sainsbury's or Co-Op where working-class women, their hair restrained by 'nets', put quarter-pounds of butter – fashioned into squares with butter-pats – and blue paper bags of sugar on to a weighted scale. When my mother paid the bill, in pounds, shillings and pence, while she might exchange pleasantries with the cashier in her glass booth she was greeted with no flippant command to 'take care', no programmed injunction to 'have a nice day'. For the 'housewife' 'nice days' merged one into the other, caring for husband and children and carrying out domestic chores. There were a few holidays, often to the same beach-hut at the same seaside where kites would be flown and beach cricket – stumps hammered into the shifting sands – was played. 'Abroad' was another country, and the 'package tour' had yet to evolve. At home the solitary Bakelite telephone, sited on the ubiquitous 'hall-table', was a fixture, and if you wanted to make a call you dialled the first three letters of the appropriate exchange: AVEnue (City of London), BALham (Tooting), AMBassador (Paddington), MAYfair (Mayfair) and so on followed by a four-digit number. For 'trunk' or long-distance (expensive) calls, you requested that the 'operator' connect you, manually, aware that when she had nothing better to do she would listen to, and sometimes contribute to, your conversation.

While in the year I was born Virginia Woolf, in her diaries, stressed the revolutionary importance for women of 'a room of one's own', in our stuccoed house in our dreaming suburb I shared a bedroom with my younger sister, bathed in the fashionably green family bathroom and took my turn to use the single lavatory across the landing with its 'pull' chain flush. The concept of 'en-suite' bathrooms was yet to arrive.

I was a sickly child and remain in questionable health to this day. Nothing is more punitive than to give a disease a meaning – invariably moralistic – or to suggest that nature is taking revenge on a godless world. For the Greeks, disease could be gratuitous or deserved (as when it was visited on one for a personal fault), a collective transgression or a crime of one's ancestors, while Thomas Mann, author of *The Magic Mountain*, suggested that disease was 'a disguised manifestation of the power of love'. Disease as a punishment is widespread in literature, and according to Susan Sontag, who wrote *Illness as Metaphor*, 'patients who are instructed that they have, unwittingly, caused their disease are also made to feel that they have deserved it'. In the late sixteenth and the seventeenth centuries it was considered that 'the happy man would not get the plague', while Adolf Hitler accused European Jews of producing a racial tuberculosis and equated them to a cancer that must be excised.

When I was four years old my tonsils were removed by our family doctor – who wore a black jacket and pin-striped trousers – as I lay on the kitchen table. I remember to this day the pungent and sickly smell of the anaesthetic administered on one of my father's large white handkerchiefs for which I was held firmly down and tricked into believing that the ether I was forced to inhale was some exotic perfume. The ensuing ice-cream, after I had been parted from my tonsils and had come round, was no compensation for the trauma of the arcane procedure. My fifth year saw tubercular glands surgically removed from my neck (this time in a 'nursing home') followed by the removal of what was, more than likely, a perfectly healthy appendix. Two ear infections requiring minor surgery, four pregnancies (followed by dilatation and curettage for ensuing haemorrhages), surgical extraction of wisdom teeth, a hysterectomy (for infection) and laparotomy (for consequent abdominal adhesions) were followed by a breast lumpectomy to remove a fibroadenoma, and Ramsay Hunt syndrome – which entailed the excision of the *chorda tympany* – which came out of the blue and resulted in seventh nerve palsy and a unilaterally paralysed face, the unflattering effects of which I have to cope with to this day. An acute intestinal obstruction (when a loop of gut becomes twisted around a strand of post-operative scar tissue) was treated conservatively in the now bulldozed Middlesex Hospital – three weeks in bed fed by means of a nasal-gastro drip – and this was followed by follicular lymphoma (a life-threatening cancer in the lung requiring both chemo- and radiotherapy). A 'Scarf and Weil' operation (involving six months' convalescence) on my foot, the onset of peripheral neuropathy, which affects my balance and mobility, vascular Parkinsonism, degenerative hip joints and osteoarthritis were visited on me for good measure. My memoir *Life Is a Joke*, published in 2013, was a cynical affirmation that my life has not always been amusing, although I continue – when I am able – to regard it as funny. You take what is dished out, and my one consolation is that I am able to lose myself in writing to 'banish the disagreeables', as Keats expressed it.

The first ten years of what I am assured has been a 'long life' – although it has fled by and doesn't seem that long to me – were informed by writers such as Pearl Buck, John Steinbeck and Ivy Compton-Burnett; artists as disparate as Picasso, Marc Chagall and Salvador Dalí; and movie legends such as Greta Garbo, as well as the rise of camps as incongruent as Butlin's (holiday) and Nazi (concentration).

Although it is hard to imagine, in the 'olden days' we managed to subsist without seatbelts, frozen food, microwave ovens, cling-film, instant coffee, email, television or mobile phones. There were no disposable nappies, tumble-dryers, electric blankets, milk cartons, fish-fingers nor soft toilet paper (scratchy rolls of brown Bronco were *de rigueur*), and space travel was light-years away. With no internet, ballpoint pens or Post-It notes, writers sat before their typewriters and tried to remember to insert the carbon (copy) paper between the pristine white sheets of A4.

At school, in common with the other girls, I wore a 'liberty bodice' with suspenders and rubber buttons attached to support my thick lisle stockings, until this was replaced by the ubiquitous 'roll-on', a kind of lesser corset, the presumed 'need' for which – I was thin as the proverbial rake – persisted for many years. In the years before the liberation provided by the commercial 'tampon' – which nervous mothers assumed would interfere with their daughters' virginity – menstruation, which was not discussed and certainly not in front of the male members of the family, was left for women to deal with as best they could. Although hardly convenient and requiring a belt to keep it in place, the so-called 'disposable' sanitary towel meant monthly embarrassments for women and girls condemned to wear cumbersome pads between their legs which inhibited their movements and which they imagined, erroneously, were visible to outside eyes. Selling the revolutionary tampon did not prove easy. Pharmacists, then mainly men, balked at stocking such intimate items, and a number of churchmen joined the mothers and denounced the innovation as destroying evidence of maidenhood. Sales did not pick up until the mid-1930s when an advertising campaign in the USA reached 45 million women, and Tampax – which liberated women from the inconvenient aspect of their monthly traumas – swiftly became available in a hundred countries.

In the doctor's surgeries, with no ancilliary help, and no 'practice managers', single-handed GPs worked from morning till night (and often during the night) to care for up to 3,000 patients, frequently dispensing their own medicines, writing 'sick-notes' and death certificates and performing minor surgery with instruments that had to be sterilized in autoclaves. They gave advice over the incessantly ringing telephone, managed their 'visits' or 'house-calls' between morning and evening surgeries, while attempting to keep pace with medical innovations, and making time to hear out the drug-company 'reps' who sat patiently in their waiting-rooms.

As the twentieth century progressed, to be punctuated by the horrors of the Second World War, the start of which saw the German invasion and occupation of Czechoslovakia and Poland, family life in England was turned upside down, and childhood, as I knew it, came to an abrupt end.

Watching the streetwise adolescents of today with their mobile devices (and sometimes their guns and their knives), their easy access to further education through government funding, their carefree sex lives, their kaleidoscope of partnerships and late marriages (if they bother with the antediluvian convention at all), their liberal gender assignations, their contempt for authority, their rejection of religion and disregard of parents and teachers, I wonder, in common with other 'oldies', whether the world has progressed since 'our day' or whether we have taken two steps forward and one step back.

24

SOLITUDE AND LONELINESS

I wandered lonely as a cloud
That floats on high o'er vales and hills,
When all at once I saw a crowd,
A host, of golden daffodils.

– William Wordsworth

Solitude has been defined as 'being alone without being lonely'. Many people enjoy solitude, a human situation in which you are your own company. It has the double advantage of being with yourself but not being with others. It should not be confused with 'loneliness' – in which you long for the presence of a particular person, spouse, sibling, best friend – or 'social isolation', when one has no shared network nor particular group of friends. You can be lonely in a crowded room without being socially isolated.

Loneliness can be 'chronic', feeling 'cut off' from others all the time; 'transient', an uncomfortable sensation that comes and goes; or 'situational', occurring only at times such as weekends, bank holidays, family gatherings or Christmas, when everyone other than you seems to be having a good time. Chronic loneliness can be a life-threatening condition. It is associated with increased risk of stroke and cardiovascular disease (to which lonely people are prone) as well as to a higher incidence of raised blood pressure, obesity and alcohol abuse. Anxiety, depression, digestive disorders and insomnia are also more prevalent among those who live alone and have no one except themselves (or possibly a goldfish) to talk to.

Writers, artists and other creative people need solitude as other people need sleep. Being by themselves and accessing their inner world, while still feeling valued and connected, has many benefits. While 'positive' solitude can help people discover their true identity and access their *moi profond* without outside distractions, 'negative' or 'imposed', solitude is involuntary and undesired at the time it occurs. The poet Philip Larkin saw life 'more as an affair diversified by company than as an affair of company diversified by solitude'. An idea can be sparked in company, but its expression takes place in solitude. If the writer or artist is silent for a long time, people and places just appear in their minds.

The 'solitary' person has no regrets, sadness or depression and is able to work, think or rest secure in the knowledge that he will not be disturbed and that no one will tread on his dreams. The word *solitude* assumes that you want nothing more than to be away from everyone or everything and that you are by yourself because you wish to be.

William Wordsworth found walking alone bliss, but then he had the company of the daffodils, ten thousand of them, 'fluttering and dancing in the breeze', to nourish and sustain his 'inward eye'. Not all of us are lucky enough to have either inward eyes or daffodils, and for many people lack of contact with other human beings is the worst-case scenario.

While for some people isolation is a result of the inability to interact with those around them, for others it is the *sine qua non* that opens the floodgates of creativity. In constant company the imagination can be stifled. Solitude helps one to discover one's identity without any outside distractions and provides time for contemplation, personal growth and self-examination. Its ramifications can be avoided as long as the solitary person knows that at the end of the day he or she has someone to come home to or a meaningful relationship with peers.

While both solitude and loneliness are characterized by 'social isolation', the resemblance ends there. Loneliness is a negative state, marked by a sense of segregation and the feeling that something, or someone, is missing, even when one is surrounded by other people. Solitude is the state of being alone but being content with one's own company and *without* feeling isolated. Solitude can be used for inner scrutiny and for growth and enjoyment. It is conducive to reflection and a positive state of engagement with oneself which provides wonderful and sufficient company. Reading requires solitude, as does contemplation of the world around us in which one can experience a state of peace and inner harmony. Solitude gives us the opportunity to enrich and replenish our lives and is a means of enjoying a quiet space from which to draw sustenance.

Although we may differ temperamentally in the amount of solitude we need, we can all benefit from tranquil periods that give us space and time to explore and to know ourselves better, to regain perspective and to take control of our lives rather than abandoning them to external forces. Solitude restores us, whereas loneliness – often marked by a painful sense of isolation – diminishes us.

Enforced loneliness or 'solitary confinement' has been a method of punishment throughout history and is used as a form of torture. It has been shown in animal studies to cause psychosis. In 'emotional' isolation one has a well-functioning social network but still feels oneself to be remote from others.

While solitude is beneficial for creativity and self-development, too much isolation can have negative effects such as have been observed in prisoners, whose behaviour might worsen, and in schoolchildren, who may react negatively. Children are generally not alone by choice, but 'social segregation' may occur when a child is unsure of how to interact with others, which can lead to shyness or social rejection. Teenagers who keep themselves to themselves find it less easy to socialize than those who balance solitude with social time.

In religious contexts solitude can be a source of genuine pleasure. Some saints embraced silence and found delight in their preferred uniformity with God. The Buddha attained enlightenment through meditation and deprivation of sensory input, bodily necessities and social interaction. The context of solitude is 'attainment of pleasure from within', but this does not always mean complete detachment from the outside world.

While introverts may avail themselves of solitude to recharge their batteries, the socially apathetic may use it as an excuse to get on with solitary chores.

Isolation is universally used as a punishment for those accused of serious crimes, for those who may be in danger of taking their own lives or for those detainees unable to participate in prison activities owing to sickness or injury. Psychiatric institutions may prescribe full or partial isolation for certain inmates – usually the violent or subversive – in order to address their particular needs and to protect the other patients.

While 'solitude' – from the Latin 'solitudinem' (loneliness) – does not always mean that one is lonely, the implication is that one enjoys one's own company. As the world spins ever faster and social media travels millions of miles in fractions of seconds, we mortals need to find new ways to cope with what may be overwhelming pressures and the feeling that we will never catch up with ourselves. We need to maintain a balance and restore some sense of being in charge of our own lives. Is 'solitude' – a time for reflection in which you are able to provide yourself with wonderful and sufficient company – the answer, and is it even acknowledged as a state of 'being' by those dependent on external sources to legitimize their existence?

We all need periods of solitude to give us time to explore and to know ourselves better. It is the counterpoint to intimacy and allows us to have a 'self' worthy of sharing. Solitude, in reasonable doses, gives us a chance to regain perspective. It allows us to take charge of our own lives and puts into perspective the unceasing bombardment of external challenges.

Loneliness, which depletes one's resources, is imposed by others; solitude is a matter of choice.

25

TRAVEL

Travel makes one modest. You see what a tiny
place you occupy in the world.

– Gustave Flaubert

In my childhood, prolonged by the Second World War when
travel to Europe was not an option, family holidays were spent
at the English seaside, not far from Margate, on the Kent coast,
where the miles of pristine sands encouraged such simple pleasures as cricket (for the benefit of my father and older brother),
'catch' with a rubber ball bought new each year from a shop
bedecked with brightly coloured buckets, spades and fishing
nets and the construction of intricate sandcastles with turrets
and moats, expunged each evening by the incoming tide.

These simple pleasures, with breaks for 'paste' sandwiches
in the hired beach hut outside which my mother sat in her
striped deckchair and where the kettle was permanently on,
were interspersed with visits to 'Dreamland' the renowned but
dilapidated funfair where illicit hours and pocket-money were
spent 'rolling pennies' (in the hope of winning more pennies)
and fishing for ducks in attempts to land a lucky number. It
was not the most sophisticated of seaside resorts, but we were
not sophisticated children. These family holidays were taken
in August when the wind frequently blew and it often rained.

They in no way prepared me for 'abroad' which came shortly after 'peace in our time' and the advent of my own family.

'Life is but a journey; to travel is to live twice,' said Omar Khayyám. I am no intrepid traveller, but constrained for so long, like greyhounds in the starting-box, my husband and I had no compunction, once a year, in leaving our demanding lives and our growing quiver of children with their two sets of extremely competent and willing grandparents (baby-minders) while we dipped our toes into the melting pot of the world, fortunately before the arrival of the ubiquitous 'package tour'. It seems unbelievable now that you could walk, without booking or queuing in the heat of the Italian sun, into the Uffizi Gallery, with its Titians and Botticellis, or relax in the tranquil Boboli Gardens where we were practically the only visitors there.

Where to begin? Every Christmas our travels took us to the awesome palette of the Grand Canyon painted in awesome colours by the dawn, to the cauldron that was Death Valley, to the crocodile-infested Everglades, to the outpost of Key West and the erstwhile homes of James Audubon with its orchids and tropical foliage, and of novelist Ernest Hemingway. I have swum in the tepid waters of the Great Barrier Reef – where the coral is now sadly being bleached by the effects of global warming – sunbathed (*pace*, Elizabeth Taylor) in Puerto Vallarta, crunched the packed snow in Finland and marvelled at the indigenous geysers of Iceland. I have enjoyed the undemanding pleasures of New Zealand from Auckland to Queenstown, been awed by the sight of Kilimanjaro, gawped at Table Mountain and quailed before

the Himalayas; I have sea-planed from Juno to the Alaskan gla-
ciers and helicoptered over the Iguassu Falls; I have been jostled
by crowds in Kathmandu, survived a cyclone in Mauritius and
fled to Kenya with its game parks and star-studded skies. I have
watched pink flamingoes standing on their single legs in Tanzania,
shed tears before the Taj Mahal, ascended Massada and traversed
the Holy City. I have sailed the Red Sea to the lost city of Petra
and visited China in the days when the roads of Beijing were
eerily empty, the shops bare, the last meal of the day was served
at five in the afternoon (after which nothing could be had to
eat), there were crumbs (if not mice) beneath the bed, students
sniggered at our 'large' English noses and the *lingua franca* was
'football'. In a grim post-war Moscow we tried, unsuccessfully,
to shake off our 'minders' who followed our every move and
crept guiltily into the bedroom at night beneath the beady eyes
of the 'babushka', in her copious scarves, who guarded the hotel
corridor. I have been a passenger in an aircraft struck by light-
ning (a scary experience), been mugged for my purse in Sienna
(where I fought off my assailant with an umbrella), been
bounced round a ship's cabin in a Force 10 gale and targeted as
a moveable feast by a variety of voracious insects. I have travelled
to Egypt and Thailand, to Budapest and Boston, to Singapore
and Rampur, to Malta and Gibraltar, to the fjords of Oslo and
the Highlands of Scotland. I have seen Slovakia and Slovenia,
Spain and Sardinia, Corsica and Croatia, Denmark and
Dubrovnik. I have made remarkable friends and curated
remarkable albums of photographs taken in places as far afield
as Vietnam, with its chilling reminders of Agent Orange, and
the killing fields of Cambodia, with its awe-inspiring Angkor

Wat, the largest religious monument in the world, which took the twelfth-century King Suryavamen thirty years to construct.

If the above list is random it is because I have no sense of direction and have been known to confuse left with right and north with south. Luckily there were always three of us on our travels, including me and the Nikon. While I frequently grew impatient as the state-of the-art camera was lovingly primed and the tripod set up, I have lived to appreciate a lasting and – non-digital – record of our many, many journeys which ended up, appropriately and less energetically, amid the white sands, the languid seas and the wild orchids of the Caribbean.

It was not all holiday. In my headier days I travelled for work. In New York – where I was booked in by the movie studios (which had optioned one of my books) to an up-market hotel facing Central Park – I could not, naively, understand why the front desk insisted on knowing my mother's maiden name, nor why the iron-coiffed, talon-nailed producer with whom I had come to work on my screenplay identified me in the early morning with the brusque enquiry 'Are you my breakfast?'

I was in New York again, in the heat of an August, when everyone in his right mind had left the city, to research my novel *Rose of Jericho* and later on spent time in Poland where my play *An Eligible Man* was playing to packed houses. Although I did not understand a word the actors were saying, the obvious delight and copious laughter of the full house indicated that the evening was a success. At the time of writing the play is still in the repertoire, and the Polish translator, who comes yearly with her family to visit me in the UK, has become a close friend.

It was some years ago that I spent time in France to explore the wine business in Bordeaux for my novel *Vintage*, commissioned by Channel 4 as a television series but later to bite the dust. For several heady weeks I was the guest of M. Anthony Barton (Château Longoa-Barton), Mme Sylvie Cazes-Regimbeau (Château Lynch-Bages) and M. Pierre-Gilles Gromand d'Every (Château de Lamarque) among many other château owners anxious to see their vineyards on television.

While the above travel was specifically 'work' orientated, everything she does and sees is grist to the writer's mill, and the typewriter or computer in her head is clacking away all the time. No experience is ever wasted, and every overheard conversation or face-to-face encounter is put to good use. There comes a time in life, however, when leaving the comfort of one's home loses its appeal, when the lure of 'foreign' parts with their bell-towers and their churches, their art and their artefacts, their suns and their siestas is outweighed by no longer having to pack a case, to prejudge the weather, to assess the 'smart' against the 'warm', to remember the sunscreen, to turn off the heating and cancel the newspapers, to water the plants and close the blinds and to email your itinerary to those who care. Apart from short stays in the English countryside, courtesy of family and friends, it is by a trick of fate – there is a splendid new hotel there overlooking my childhood sands – that I go back to Margate where, after years of dereliction amongst the boarded-up shops, the new Dreamland with its Big Wheel and its karaoke, its 'gourmet' candy floss and £18 million renovation, has risen from the ashes and the new Turner Contemporary Gallery beckons.

My touring days are over, and my preferred form of travel, like that of Gustave Flaubert, now that the years have caught up with me, would be to 'lie on a divan and have the scenery carried past'.

26

ANGER

I am awfully greedy; I want everything from
life. I want to be a woman and to be a man,
to have many friends and to have loneliness,
to work much and write good books, to travel and
enjoy myself, to be selfish and to be unselfish . . .
You see, it is difficult to get all which I want. And
then when I do not succeed I get mad
with anger.

– Simone de Beauvoir

Anger, is a normal human emotion. It varies in intensity from
irritation to fury and is a typical response to the feeling that
one is being attacked or treated unfairly. Everyone gets angry
on occasion. It is not always a bad response and can, in fact,
be useful. It is only when one's angry feelings get out of control that they can become destructive and make one feel at the
mercy of sensations one is unable to handle.

This highly emotional state can vary from momentary irritation – someone takes the chocolate biscuit you had your eye on
– to frustration and rage when you are pipped at the post to the
last parking space and are going to be late for an appointment.
Like other overpowering feelings, anger gives rise to physiological and biological changes, such as a rise in blood pressure and
an increased heart rate.

Anger can be the result of both internal and external circumstances. It can be directed at a specific person, arise from brooding about one's day-to-day problems or by dwelling on memories of past traumatic events. While logic will often defeat anger, anger, even when justified, can quickly become irrational. The instinctive way to respond to it is with aggression. Those with a low anger threshold are more likely to do this, but a number of strategies can be used to manage angry feelings: taking a deep breath, expressing one's feelings, trying to calm down and verbalizing one's needs are all ways of averting confrontation. Unexpressed anger can lead to obstructive behaviour such as 'getting one's own back' at someone without telling them why or by hostility. We all know people who constantly put others down, are hyper-critical and make cynical remarks. They have not learned how to express their anger constructively, and it comes as no surprise that they find it difficult either to make relationships or to keep friends.

A certain amount of anger is necessary to survival, and the instinctive way to express this is to respond belligerently. It would be unreasonable, however, to lash out at everyone who happens to irritate or annoy us. 'Listening' to what is being said can keep a situation from escalating, and expressing oneself in an assertive, non-belligerent manner is the best way to get hostile feelings under control. In order to do this one has to make clear what one's needs are. This does not mean being pushy or demanding but being respectful of both oneself and of others.

Unexpressed anger can lead to 'passive-aggressive' behaviour, getting back at people without telling them why, rather than confronting them head on. Learning to control not only 'outward' behaviour but 'internal' responses will ensure that nobody gets hurt. Some people are more prone to anger than others. They are quick to lose their cool and often curse and throw things. Others may be perpetually irritable and grumpy, withdraw socially, sulk or make themselves physically ill. Those with a low anger threshold often come from disruptive families that are not skilled at emotional communication.

People who use their anger as a licence to hurt others do nothing either to help themselves or to avoid confrontation. Greater insight will enable them to find out what it is that makes them angry and to develop tactics that prevent situations from escalating.

Those who are prone to anger generally have a low tolerance for frustration which encompasses minor inconveniences and petty annoyances. Unable to take things in their stride, they become irritated when they are held to account for minor infractions or inconsequential mistakes. While it may be therapeutic to 'let it all hang out', research shows that this approach only escalates resentment and does nothing to help either the one who is angry or the target of his antagonism. A more successful way of dealing with the problem is to find out what sparks one's annoyance and to develop ways of keeping these triggers from tipping one over the edge. Techniques such as relaxation therapy, deep breathing and yoga – recommended by the experts for both parties in a volatile relationship – are all advocated to soothe angry feelings. Changing the way they think (Cognitive Restructuring) can help those who tend to curse, swear or speak in exaggerated or dramatic terms to behave more rationally.

Logic will always defeat anger, because anger, even when justified, can quickly become irrational. Putting matters into perspective and not jumping to conclusions – generally things are not as bad as they seem – will often avoid the frustration experienced by the angry person when he is unable to get what he wants. By facing one's anger head on, thinking through one's responses and not saying the first thing that comes into one's head, one is less likely to lose patience with a problem that does not get solved immediately. It is natural to get defensive in the face of criticism, but if one actually *listens* to what is being said and resists the temptation to fight back the situation can usually be prevented from escalating. This will result in a gratifying sense of achievement.

Cognitive restructuring may change the way that one thinks by replacing negative thoughts – 'everything is in ruins' – by positive ones, such as that what has taken place is not 'the end of the world'. If one reminds oneself that 'the world is not out to get you' each time hostile feelings arise, a more balanced perspective will ensue. When angry people don't get what they want frustration can transmute into fury. It is more useful to change one's demands than to insist on these demands be met. It is natural to become defensive in the face of criticism. If one stops to think what is informing the criticism, however, and manages to resist fighting back, it will prevent confrontation escalating and stop the situation getting out of control.

Humour can often be of use. Refusing to take the situation – or oneself – seriously and avoiding sarcasm (thinly disguised aggression) will often lighten a situation and diffuse hostile feelings. Angry responses can also be minimized by avoiding stressful encounters and by making the effort to change the way that one thinks. In the very worst scenario, where anger is out of control, therapists specializing in 'anger management' are there to help clients diffuse rage and cope with uncontrollable anger.

Look Back in Anger, John Osborne's strongly autobiographical play, based on and inspired by the author's disastrous marriage to actress Pamela Lane, was, according to the playwright, written in seventeen passionate days while sitting in a deckchair on Morecombe Pier. Premièred at the Royal Court in 1956, with its coruscating language and cruel depiction of 'ordinary' people, it revolutionized London's theatre and left audiences gasping. In the course of the action Jimmy Porter, literature's seminal example of an 'angry young man', rants at the social and political structures he believes have kept him from achieving his post-war dreams and aspirations. His vituperative tirades are directed against the prevailing smugness of the middle classes, women in general and in particular his wife Alison – played by Osborne's future wife Mary Ure – who appears to have 'taken on the nation's laundry' and is permanently chained to her iconic ironing-board. Porter's anger, culminating in a vituperative outburst such as had never before been witnessed on the London stage, references Osborne's earlier life when, at the age of ten, he witnessed the death of his beloved father. The protagonist's violent flare-ups shocked critics and audiences, and, as the play progresses, Jimmy, who becomes more and more vituperative, transfers his contempt for his upper-middle-class impassive wife to her haughty best friend Helena. Hearing that Alison has invited Helena to stay compounds Jimmy's rage, and conflict soon becomes inevitable as the 'escapist' theatre that characterized the previous generation is replaced by the harshness of new 'dramatic realism'.

The viciousness of Jimmy Porter's unprovoked attacks, on both the times in general and women in particular, culminates in catastrophic results not the least of which is the premature birth and subsequent loss of Alison's baby.

While most reviews of the play were deeply negative – 'unspeakably dirty and squalid' – the highly respected theatre critic Kenneth Tynan described the first 'kitchen-sink drama' as a 'minor miracle' and said that 'he could not love anyone who did not wish to see it'. With its drift towards anarchy and rejection of received attitudes, Osborne's cutting-edge play said more about anger and its fall-out than can be found in many treatises on human behaviour. Had there then been such a thing as 'anger management', more understanding of the current drift towards the left and the automatic rejection of 'official attitudes', this landmark piece might neither have had its audiences reeling with shock, nor seen the light of day. Prickly and paranoid, Jimmy Porter's rage is aimed at the social and political structures that he believes have kept him from achieving his potential. His jeering hostility is directed towards his friends and, in particular, towards his long-suffering wife. (Osborne had himself feuded his way through no less than five marriages.) He uses the examples of the Second World War, the development of the atom bomb and the decline of the British Empire to demonstrate how an entire civilization had lost the innocence that previous generations were able to maintain. Jimmy's festering resentment is an attempt to rouse those around him from their cultural apathy. As the depressed and alcoholic playwright points out so coherently in this ground-breaking anti-Establishment play, he feels both that he is entitled to sympathy and that he has every reason to be angry.

27

TRUTH AND BEAUTY

Everyone sees who I appear to be but only a few
know the real me. You only see what I choose to
show. There's so much behind my smile you just
don't know.

– Anonymous

The first thing to know about truth is that it is unchangeable,
ageless and constant. It does not vary or shift and is a piece of
unalterable reality, a state of mind which is an accurate reflection of things in existence. Truth is the same for all of us, and it
is untrue to say that 'what is true for you is not true for me',
although different people have different *interpretations* of truth,
which many are inclined to stretch. According to the dictionary,
truth is defined as 'an idea that is accepted by most people as
being true', but this, of course, depends on individual percep-
tions. What seems right for me is not always right for you.

Henry James's very obvious truth was that 'the deepest quality of a work of art will always be the quality of the mind of the
producer. No good novel ever proceeded from a superficial mind.'

Truth is what one wants to believe, and, as one gets more
mature or more educated, one's opinions change. What seems
true at eighteen may no longer be true at eighty. Society fluctu-
ates, and one's view of 'truth' can be influenced by where you
live and to what social class you belong. While many people

today – and not only the disadvantaged – believe it is OK to engage in drugs, alcohol and promiscuous sex, others regard these activities as wrong, because they have been taught the 'truth' about them by parents, siblings and friends. As one grows older one's perspective changes, and one must decide for oneself whether the conclusions one has arrived at are right or wrong, true or false.

Truth can be many things to many people, but once someone has decided that his or hers is the 'real' truth it is difficult for that person to change his or her mind, and views on what is true and what is untrue may become entrenched. Truth founded on religion is based on whichever faith one happens to have been born into. Once someone has discovered the 'truth' in a particular religion it is extremely difficult for that individual to alter his or her feelings about that religion, and this can take many forms, from the extremes of praising a particular god every hour to getting physically involved – through acts of charity – with the poor and needy.

There can be no examination of the truth without citing the Cretan Paradox, or 'false premise', and the illogicality of 'Pinocchio's nose'. The first states, 'Epimenides the Cretan says that all Cretans are liars', but Epimenides was himself a Cretan, therefore he is himself a liar and his statement is false. Since Pinocchio's nose grows whenever he tries to say something that is not true, the paradox about his nose assumes that all lies about the future turn out to be false. Whether it does turn out to be true is irrelevant, since the growth of his nose hinges on the intention, rather than the result. He could therefore say, 'My nose will grow', believing it will not grow since he believes there is a link between his telling a lie and his nose growing. He could therefore assume that his nose will grow when saying something false. He would, of course, be telling the truth, and his nose would not grow. This would make him wrong but would not mean that he was a liar. The paradox conflates lies with errors or falsity, and therefore its assumption is incorrect.

Truth, in some cases, is what one wants to 'believe' is true and in other cases what one truly 'knows' is true. Various echelons of society have diverse views on truth which can mean different things to different people. However, once someone's mind has been set on the 'real' version of the truth it can be extremely hard for that person to alter it.

When in 1819 poet John Keats wrote 'Ode on a Grecian Urn' declaring that 'Beauty is truth, truth beauty, – that's all Ye know on earth, and all ye need to know' he put the cat among the pigeons as far as his critics were concerned, and it is rather in spite of than because of them that the verses have survived. The critic Andrew Bennett complained of 'the lack of a definite voice of the urn causes the reader to question who is really speaking these words, to whom they are speaking, and what is meant by the words', and the poet Robert Bridges believed that the final lines redeemed an otherwise bad poem to which Arthur Quiller-Couch countered that they were a 'a vague observation . . . an uneducated conclusion'. T.S. Eliot in 1929 weighed in with the observation that the lines were 'a serious blemish on a beautiful poem. The statement of Keats seems to me meaningless; or perhaps the fact that it is grammatically meaningless conceals another meaning from me.'

For some philosophers, truth corresponds with reality and is a simple matter of 'telling it like it is'; it is the way things really are, and any other viewpoint is incorrect. It is acceptable to say 'this is true' as long as it is not followed by 'and therefore that is false'. This is especially true in matters of faith and religion where every belief system is supposedly on equal footing.

A teacher facing a class may say, 'The only exit to this room is the door on the right.' Which is absolutely true from where he or she is standing. For the students who sit facing her, however, the door is on the left.

Beauty lies in 'the eye of the beholder' and has been defined as 'a quality that pleases or delights the senses or the mind'. The perception of beauty is subjective and that which one person finds beautiful or admirable may not appeal to another.

Voltaire said, 'Ask a toad what is beauty and he will reply, "A female toad with two great round eyes, a large flat mount and a brown back."'

While there is a basic human instinct, an internal appreciation, for harmony, balance and rhythm (which can be defined as beauty), the experience of beauty is a judgement of a subjective but common human truth. Tolstoy's Levin in *Anna Karenina*. 'did not like talking and hearing about the beauty of nature . . . words for him detracted from the beauty of what he saw'.

Someone banging on about a particular panorama or sunset will soon cause the listener to pull up the drawbridge.

Levin says, 'Always coming into raptures over nature is to betray poverty of the imagination. Compared with what my imagination can offer me, all these streams and cliffs are absolute rubbish, nothing else.'

Beauty in art relies on what the viewer feels on a conscious or base-instinct level, and much of what we consider to be beautiful is based on our genetics or environment. A person becomes beautiful if they win the genetic lottery and is physically appealing to other human beings. How desirable another person will be is, on some level, based on one's own sexual drive and instincts. A fit male body is physically attractive, while large breasts and wide hips in women are indicators of a potentially good mother. For centuries women have been judged initially – by both men and other women – for their looks, which puts those females with delightful personalities but less alluring physical attributes at a disadvantage. Regardless of personality or level of intelligence, a man's initial impression of a woman is based on her appearance, and the media promotes the idea that women must conform with the 'Barbie' image in order to be found desirable. A tall, young, white female with firm breasts, slim hips, shapely legs and long blonde hair is more likely to receive attention from men than someone who does not fit this blueprint. With this image of how they are 'supposed' to look in their minds, impressionable adolescent girls struggle to attain the current definition of 'beauty'. Some of them, perpetually dissatisfied with their appearance, will become anorexic or bulimic, conditions which are hard to cure and which can be fatal if not recognized and treated early. Artificially inflated lips, 'boob' jobs, liposuction, the stapling of stomachs or hazardous levels of dieting are some of the ways in which young women attempt to fit the mould that society has designated for them. Colluding with this vulnerable sector, the beauty industry thrives on a woman's wish to be perceived as 'pleasing' and every year creates an increasing and ever-changing amount of merchandise designed to enhance their looks. The marketing of these seductively packaged and widely promoted lotions and potions leads women, particularly those with body dysmorphia, to believe that if they use these products they will become more desirable, thus conforming to society's idea of attractiveness.

While in the past risky 'procedures' were available only to the wealthy, alterations to physical appearance are now available to a wider market. In the mistaken belief that 'nips and tucks' will enhance their looks – and by extension their lives – women and young girls obsessed with 'body image' (and who can afford it) 'lift' their faces, augment their breasts, remove excess skin from eyelids and necks and superfluous fat from their bellies. While the aim of what, to all intents and purposes, is 'major surgery' is to help them conform to what society deems pleasing, what they are actually doing is mutilate their bodies and line the pockets of the cosmetic surgeons in a futile effort to repair their malfunctioning psyches.

Is 'truth' simply a matter of telling it how it is, and 'beauty' really in the eye of the beholder? The debate continues.

28

CARING

Caring: the work or practice of looking after
those unable to care for themselves, especially
on account of age or illness.

– *Oxford English Dictionary*

As the population ages, a new and indispensable workforce
has surfaced in the so-called First World countries. As if from
nowhere, a veritable army of Jasons and Husseins, of Mimis
and Lanas, of Angelos and Jessa-Maes has arisen to tend to the
needs of an increasingly elderly population, more and more of
whom are mentally or physically challenged. Known as 'carers',
a syllogism which has crept into the English language, the appellation covers both a band of angels who treat their clients with
the compassion they would lavish on members of their own
families, and a – fortunately small – number of psychopaths to
whom the vulnerable are fair game.

Those carers employed by our ailing National Health Service, in receipt of the minimum wage and on zero-hours
contracts, no matter how well motivated, have the most thank-
less task of all, and it is hardly surprising that more than 900 of
them quit their jobs every day. With far too many home visits
on their rotas, they set off in their clapped-out cars, on foot or by
erratic public transport, in all weathers, to streets and districts

with which they are unfamiliar. Having located and arrived at the destination entered on their worksheets, they are instructed to ring the doorbell – if the patient is ambulant – or to punch in a code on a special keypad attached to the door jamb which will allow them access to those who are bedridden or otherwise incapable of admitting them. The next fifteen minutes– ten in some overstretched boroughs – are crucial. Confronting a fragile and elderly man or woman forced by necessity and disability to lie, sometimes for hours, in a soiled bed, the carer has the choice of changing the sheets and putting them in the washing-machine (if there is one), bathing the patient to make him or her more comfortable or preparing and feeding him or her a light meal and administering a little tender loving care before completing the paperwork and getting to the next port of call. These are heart-rending decisions. Is fifteen minutes really all our National Health Service, once the envy of the world, can afford? Must the elderly and infirm go unwashed, hungry and confused about their medication, to languish in soiled sheets until the next flying visit from a kaleidoscope of professionals whose ever-changing names are not worth remembering? Is that really the best we can manage?

Money matters. Those patients who can afford private agency fees, or who have access to 'Hospice at Home' which provides a 'free' end-of-life care service to those lucky enough to qualify for it, are looked after by a rota of carers with hard-to-recall names and varying ethnicity. For some incomprehensible reason 'caring' is not a job for the British. Obese and skinny, short and tall, young and old, fluent – to a greater or lesser degree – in English, this altruistic army hales from every corner of the globe. Many have left children behind in their native countries to be looked after by relatives to whom almost every penny of their salaries finds its way. While their abandoned families occupy their waking thoughts, the carers rarely speak of them. Bringing comfort to the sick and elderly, uncomplainingly feeding and washing them, checking their oxygen supplies, administering their medication and dressing their pressure sores secures the futures of the Filipino, Sri Lankan, Bangladeshi and Chinese children who stare uncompromisingly back at them from the well-thumbed photographs in their handbags or pockets.

The carers' tasks are manifold, and, no matter how disagreeable their work may be, this faceless army – on which the NHS and agencies with quaint names such as 'Cherry Tree' and 'Samango' depend – carries them out with varying degrees of empathy and efficiency.

Paradoxical as it may seem, it is not the most clued-up or efficient carers, those whose 'hospital corners' are the neatest, whose hyperdermic injections are painless, whose patience is inexhaustible, who are the greatest comfort to the sick, the bedridden and the housebound but those whose empathy with their patients overrides their occasionally unpredictable nursing skills.

Just such a carer was Dorabella – who came from an agency and who was much in demand – whose bed-making was erratic, who burned the toast (her grandmother in Manila had done all the cooking) and frequently forgot the nightly teeth-cleaning ritual. Despite these shortcomings, silent as the proverbial mouse, her hair in a lustrous ponytail that reached to her waist, dressed in leggings and T-shirts with risqué motifs across her childish breasts, she went about her duties. Her patients, no matter how sick, followed her every move. Unlike some of the other carers, Dorabella knew, as if by telepathy, when her charges wanted to talk and when they did not feel like speaking. She anticipated their every need and attended to their comfort. She did not wait to be told when a pillow was misplaced or when her charge had slipped awkwardly down the bed.

Night after night, after she had settled the patient and made sure that the bell – with which she could be summoned from the sofa where she slept – the torch, the bedside clock, the carafe of water, the throat sweets (in case of choking) and the box of tissues were in easy reach, Dorabella did not, unlike the other carers who were only too glad to finish their nightly shift, rush away.

Pulling up a chair she would sit by the bed and listen to her patient's stories about the past. Was it possible that this lumpen white-haired woman, eyes milky with cataracts, had once been the feisty-looking raven-haired concert pianist of the black-and-white photograph on the dressing-table? How had the circuit judge, holding sway over his court, metamorphosed into the living skeleton whose pain-racked body scarcely made a bump in the bedclothes? As night succeeded night Dorabella never tired of listening to tales about her charges' lives in happier times and telling them about her own. When their eyelids grew heavy and the drugs she had administered, according to instructions, began to do their work, she sat silently, patiently, beside them. Only her lips moved, willing her silent prayers to a deity she firmly believed in to make them well. When they were almost asleep Dorabella would lean forward and take their weightless hands, the veins etched in history, in hers. 'Good night, sleep tight, mind the bugs don't bite,' she would whisper, as if to a child. Only when their eyelids were tightly shut, their breathing regular, would she tiptoe away and glide silently, like a moonbeam, from the room.

29

SEX

I do not believe that writing or any other activity
I am capable of can exist without sex.

– Vladimir Nabokov

Sexual activity is a vital principle that connects the desires and pleasures of the body with the knowledge of human intimacy. This results in erotic love, close friendship, mating and pro-creation. Before what we now regard as 'the sexual revolution' of the 1960s –a time of rebellion against the beliefs, fashions and social mores of the previous generation when pre-marital sex became the order of the day and the idea of marriage was considered outmoded –sex was not talked about other than in hushed voices or behind closed doors; certainly not in front of the children, who were not taught about it in the classroom, other perhaps than in reference to the reproductive organs of frogs and other vertebrates. It was perhaps surprising that human offspring were conceived at all, as many teenagers left school without the slightest idea that sexual activity was a vital principle of human living or that the desires and pleasures of the body – together with a knowledge of human sexuality – resulted in erotic love, intimate friendships, mating and procreation.

While the physical and emotional aspects of sexuality include bonds between individuals, expressed through profound feelings or physical manifestations of love, for Freud (the Grandmaster) sexuality was a question of orientation and could be experienced and expressed in a variety of ways. These included thoughts, fantasies, desires and beliefs as well as physical, emotional, spiritual and social aspects.

Social characteristics are the effects of human society on one's sexuality, while spirituality concerns an individual's psychic connection with others. Sexuality also impacts, and is impacted upon, by cultural, moral, ethical and religious components of life. Although some may argue that sexuality is determined by genetics, others believe that it is moulded by the environment and maintain that both these factors interact to form an individual's sexual orientation.

Contrary to popular belief, the 'sexual revolution', a time of rebellion against the fashions and social mores of the previous generation, the freedom to have lots of sex in lots of different ways and the disregard of marriage, began not in the 1960s with the advent of the contraceptive pill (available at first only to married women), when Elvis was thrusting his hips suggestively, with Hugh Hefner's *Playboy* or the assertion of Phillip Larkin that 'sexual intercourse began in nineteen sixty-three'. Its origins were in the 1940s and 1950s when the 'silent generation', who didn't *talk* much about sex, found out about it through guilt-ridden experimentation. The truth of the matter was that the Second World War saw a liberalizing effect on values which affected everything, from child-rearing and religion to sexual mores. This left young people – who discovered to their delight that love was no longer a prerequisite for sex – morally at sea.

This 'silent generation' may have kept quiet about what they were actually up to while Dr Alfred Kinsey was conducting his famous (or infamous) study on human sexuality, but the sexual revolution – in particular the experimentation with oral sex, once considered beyond the pale if it was considered at all – was brewing and continued to brew until the wheel, was not only reinvented, but turned full circle. By the time they are ten, if not earlier, today's children are not only savvy *vis-à-vis* sexual relationships but often conversant with the acronym 'LGBTQ' (Lesbian, Gay, Bisexual, Transgender and Queer), used as shorthand for those with a non-normative gender or sexuality. Sometimes the frankness of the media, not to mention the gossip of their peer groups, is too much for young children to take on board.

What actually took place in the 1960s was not in fact a revolution but an upheaval in social conventions and the defiance of the last knockings of a moral code in which the only permissible type of sex was married, missionary and heterosexual. Overnight, or so it seemed, love was no longer a prerequisite for intimacy, marriage was regarded as *vieux jeux*, explicit sex on screen and stage became commonplace and pornography freely available. Nothing was regarded as alien and very little regarded as 'wrong'.

Today an active sex life among the young is regarded as both a necessity and a fashion accessory. It is promoted as the key to well-being, psychological vitality and healthy relationships, although, paradoxically, in some circles, sexual freedom – and by extension internet pornography – is still regarded as sinful and corrupting. This belief is apparent in the ideological battles over abortion, birth control and sexual assault. While the view that 'to have sex' is in some way an 'achievement', the compulsion to prove oneself sexually has created a new kind of guilt: that of not being sexual *enough*. Where moralists were once troubled by the belief that love justified premarital sex, such concerns no longer hold water. Love is neither a precondition for intimacy, nor intimacy a precondition for sex. 'Nothing should be seen as alien nor looked down upon as wrong.' A good sex life is regarded not only as a 'necessity' and an achievement but also the secret of good health. The view that it is also 'sinful and corrupting' is still evident in the battles over abortion and birth control, the homilies about abstinence and the current attitudes towards the victims of rape and sexual assault.

In the fifth century AD Saint Augustine declared sex to be immoral unless it was for the sole purpose of procreation within a marriage. Abstinence and celibacy signified higher spiritual devotion, and any sexual act outside the moral code was punishable. This notion of sex as sin continued in Western society, with little challenge, until the twentieth century when Freud brought issues of sexuality into the public domain. This paved the way for Alfred Kinsey who, through his extensive researches in the USA, discovered that masturbation and oral sex were more common than many people liked to admit. Rather than a 'sexual revolution' an upheaval in 'social conventions' is what actually took place.

Sexual activity is a vital principal of human living that connects the desires, pleasures and energy of the body with a knowledge of human intimacy. This results in erotic love, intimate friendship, mating and procreation. Interest in sexual activity typically increases when an individual reaches puberty and – contrary to received wisdom – can persist, albeit in various inventive guises, well into old age when, despite the obstacle of failing bodies, simply being close to a beloved partner can beget desire: the longer sexual intimacy is continued the younger one will feel inside and, according to the latest research, the over-eighties enjoy better sex than those who are middle-aged. Older people are not only more likely to share the sexual preferences of their partners but to feel more emotionally attached to them.

Opinions differ on the origins of sexual orientation. Some argue that it is determined by genetics, some that it is moulded by environment and others that these two factors merge, giving rise to the 'nature versus nurture' debate. Research into sexuality in Dinka culture, one of the largest ethnic groups in South Sudan, suggests that '10 per cent of the population has chromosomal variations that do not fit neatly into the XX-female and XY-male set of categories'.

Socio-cultural aspects of sexuality include historical developments and religious beliefs. Examples include the comprehensive Jewish views on permitted sexual pleasure within marriage, as well as other religious views on the avoidance of sexual pleasure and the sexually repressive views of some cultures.

Poets have long turned their rhetoric towards arguments for intimacy and have frequently used verse to urge their readers to further their sexual pursuits. Horace's '*carpe diem*', seize the day, encouraged love-making without further ado, while Shakespeare immortalized beauty and love, and by extension sex, in his sonnets. Robert Herrick exhorted all Romeos to 'gather ye rosebuds while ye may'. This graphic image is said to have been purloined by the screenwriter Herman J. Mankiewicz, who used the term 'rosebud' in the movie *Citizen Kane*, believed to refer to William Randolph Hearst's pet name for the most intimate part of his mistress's anatomy. For perspicacious novelist David Lodge, 'Literature is mostly about having sex and not much about having children. Life is the other way round.'

Today 'meat market' dating apps such as Tinder and Grindr have spurred a new sexual revolution and, as casual 'hook-ups' have become the norm, the popularity of 'texting', which eliminates the need for 'feeling', has taken the embarrassment out of asking someone for a date and made 'flirting' more fun. It also means that you can check someone out before deciding to meet them for a 'drink', which in some instances, in accordance with current mores, could be a synonym for, or the prelude to, sex, no longer the taboo it once was. These popular apps appeal to people who maybe have a sex drive too high to handle and who are looking to cheat on their partners and have sex with someone who likes 'kinky fun', 'erotic movies' or 'dressing up'. Since such sites attract more than 37 million users – one going as far as proclaiming 'Life is short. Have an affair' – it would be reasonable to assume that times have irrevocably changed. It is hardly surprising that two-thirds of users of these internet sites are men and that only about 3 per cent are aged over forty-five. With the decline of religion and the stigma once attached to an 'extramarital affair', there is a level of understanding, propagated by newspaper cartoonists – who paint graphic pictures of married couples sitting glumly at the breakfast table wondering if they will be found out – about why people have them.

Ageing, as well as some illnesses, medication and disability, brings physical changes in both men and women which can affect the ability to have and to enjoy sex. As men get older, impotence, or erectile dysfunction, becomes a problem which in some cases can be reversed with the sex-life-saving drug Viagra – originally designed in 1989 to help men with high blood pressure and angina – and other mechanical aids, which have prolonged the potency of many a suitor and rescued countless relationships. While sexuality is often a delicate balance of physical and emotional issues, one's *feelings* towards one's partner may affect performance, and many older couples find greater satisfaction in their sex lives than they did when they were young. They are likely to have fewer distractions, more time, more privacy, no worries about birth control and a more profound intimacy with long-standing partners. While the sexually active young may cringe at the thought of kissing and touching grandparents, perhaps they need to be disabused of the thought that sexual relationships among the elderly are weird, shocking and gross, that they no longer form a vital part of their lives and that they belong in the realms of fantasy.

Sexuality is here to stay. Be it permitted or proscribed, be it in the interests of recreation or procreation, be it the prerogative of the young or the consolation of the old, it will find a way.

30

KINDNESS

Be kind, for everyone you meet is fighting
a hard battle.

– Plato

Kindness, the practice or quality of being kind, is doing something for others without expecting them to reciprocate. It is the act of going out of your way to be nice; to show the recipient of your kindness that you care. Even if you don't. Particularly if you don't. Kindness is a self-fulfilling prophecy, and, like microbes in a petrie dish, it breeds kindness. To the surprise of many people determined to embrace kindness, whether it is an old or a new leaf you are turning over, the effort is minimal and the return, in feeling good about oneself, maximal.

There is a difference between being 'kind' and being 'nice'. A nice person, a 'people-pleaser', who wants her friends to like her, puts others before herself and takes great care not to offend them. She avoids conflict and finds it hard to say no, manipulating others in order to fulfil her own emotional needs. She wants people to think well of her and lives in a state of denial, unaware that her so-called 'good nature' may be due to the fact that, subconsciously, she is looking for approval. The 'nice' person is often insecure and must learn how to love, value and accept herself for who she is. Once she has done this she will be free from seeking appreciation from others and can choose to be kind and giving from a place of pure motives and not from fear of being rejected or a compulsion to be liked. She must learn to say 'no', politely, while letting it be known that her action is a result of considered choice rather than a desire to please.

A kind person is genuinely concerned about other people and is honest about what she thinks and feels in order to avoid conflict. She has no trouble saying 'no' politely if she doesn't want to do something or if it doesn't fit in with her schedule. She sets and maintains healthy emotional boundaries, doesn't allow people to 'walk all over her' and is honest both with herself and with others. If her motives are genuine no one will mistake her kindness for weakness.

How do you know if you are a kind person? The acid test is if someone were to pay you 50p for every kind word you uttered about people and collect 50p for every unkind word that came out of your mouth, how rich would you be? Few of us, I suspect, would be millionaires. Although we might not admit it, there is a great deal of satisfaction in dishing the dirt, either 'about' someone or 'to' someone; it feeds into our feelings of superiority and enhances the sense of inferiority to which many of us are prone. It is not only through speech that we have the option of being kind or unkind but in our actions. Which of us has not eaten lunch in a busy canteen when, from the corner of our eye, we see a lost soul with a laden tray looking for somewhere to sit? All of us need to be alone at times, but making eye contact, and indicating that there is space next to you – even if you have to move up a bit – is not only your good deed for the day but will boost your ego. There is no need to talk to the newcomer: if you do, however, the likelihood is that you will learn something not only about him or her but about yourself. There is substantial scientific evidence to the effect that being kind not only gives you a warm glow but makes both you and those around you happy:

'You cannot do a kindness too soon, for you never know how soon it will be too late,' said Ralph Waldo Emerson.

Kindness, no matter how minimal, is never wasted. Like stones thrown into a pond, every act of benevolence or consideration produces a ripple that has no rational end. The higher the degree of self-esteem the more likely one is to treat others with respect and consideration. The level of success is limited only by our imagination. 'No act of kindness is ever wasted,' said Aesop. Being a little kinder than is absolutely necessary is a good start to implementing our resolve to join the ranks of the compassionate. While not easy, the recognition of this is the beginning of wisdom. If we try always to be a little more caring, a little more sympathetic, than is absolutely essential, a kindness 'habit' will be formed, and, given time, we may abandon our ingrained selfishness and join the ranks of considerate human beings. If this sounds sanctimonious perhaps it is. It costs nothing and has positive rewards.

Many so-called 'nice' people are subconsciously looking for approval in order to boost their egos. They are dependent upon others for positive feedback and have not learned how to love, value and accept themselves for what they are. Those who are not dependent upon such approval can make a choice to be kind from a stance of pure intentions and not from fear of being rejected or a compulsion to be liked. One must learn to say 'no' and communicate the fact that one's actions are a result of choice and not of obligation; to be assertive and to stand one's ground. There's a difference between giving someone the shirt off your back and simply allowing them take it. Kindness is a personal victory. In the words of Seneca, 'Wherever there is a human being, there is an opportunity for a kindness.' When we feel upset with something someone said or did, it is a kindness – both to ourselves and to them – to bring it out into the open, to tell them about it and to discuss it. You can't change other people, and it is futile to expect any gratitude for your actions. A true act of kindness is helping someone out without putting them into your debt. This is done not to make ourselves look good but from compassion for a fellow human being. Although there is nothing wrong with feeling good about it or enjoying it, kindness is an anonymous donation, and there should be no expectation of reciprocity.

Other people's boundaries must be respected. They know what is best for them and, although it may be difficult, it can sometimes mean them saying no to you, which can leave us feeling anything but kind.

As long as we are kind to ourselves we are coming from a place where we are free to show kindness to others.

31

CUPBOARD LOVE

Cremation is the combustion, vaporization
and oxidation of dead bodies to basic chemical
compounds, such as gases, ashes and mineral
fragments retaining the appearance of dry bone.

– Wikipedia

The older one gets the more time seems to be spent in crematoria. The crematorium of choice, for north Londoners, is that
in Hoop Lane, Golders Green, one of the oldest in Britain. The
land for the crematorium was purchased in 1900 for the sum of
£6,000, and the crematorium was opened in 1902 by Sir Henry
Thompson. The tranquil gardens, with their contemplative
benches and pergolas, are included in the National Register of
Historic Parks and Gardens.

The crematorium, which is secular, accepts all faiths as well as
humanists, atheists, agnostics and other non-believers. Clients
are free to arrange their own type and order of service or – if
there is to be no service – their remembrance 'event'. While no
two cremation ceremonies are identical, there is an order to
them which reflects the preferences of the deceased and/or his
or her relatives. Hoop Lane, which must be one of the busiest
crematoria in the world, schedules its services to last thirty
minutes, or one hour, on the hour, throughout the day. As in a

military operation punctuality is key. If you arrive prematurely you will be asked, respectfully, whatever the weather, to wait in the courtyard that doubles as a car park, conversing *sotto voce* until the current service is concluded. As the sitting congregation leave by the 'exit' doors which lead to terraces strewn with colourful wreaths and bunches of flowers, the next coterie of mourners is ushered silently in through the 'entry' doors at the near end of the 'chapel' to select their seats. Family – many of whom the deceased might neither have seen nor spoken to in years – are respectfully directed to the first two rows of pews by sombre-faced staff to the accompaniment of Schubert's Ave Maria – guaranteed to bring tears to the most cynical eyes – Leonard Cohen's 'Halleluja', Chopin's *Funeral March* or whatever turned the deceased on. A grandchild playing a recorder is likely to be far more affecting than a professional musician playing the harp.

There is a shuffling hiatus while orders of service are located and the coffin on its bier, on which nobody's gaze cares to linger, is surreptitiously checked out. The personality of the incumbent is frequently revealed by the shape and composition of his or her sarcophagus: a guitar or a motor-bike; wicker or cardboard (in the interests of the planet); lovingly decorated in felt pen; adorned with informal snapshots of the inmate fishing or scaling mountains or whatever that person's obsession happened to be; polished wood, decorously adorned with signifiers of the deceased's passion, the painter's palate, the garden-lover's favourite flower.

Into the expectant silence a cleric, minister or relative, depending on the faith (or lack of) of the one who has 'passed', will welcome the congregation with opening remarks, some of which may be missed by those at the back of the hall, the acoustics at this particular crematorium not being of the best.

The eulogy of the minister – if there is one – will be followed by speeches from family and friends, after which the congregation sing or join in a reading, expressing the views of those assembled regarding life, death and mourning. 'Grieve not for me . . . Death is nothing at all.' Canon Henry Scott-Holland's popular epitaph moves the hardest of irreligious hearts. 'What is this death but a negligible accident . . . ? One brief moment and all will be as it was before – only better, infinitely happier and for ever.'

After the reading the celebrant will deliver a personal tribute to, and appreciation of, the life of the departed, following which there will be more music before a quiet time for reflection, prayer or words of comfort. The service will conclude with a verse recited in unison (many request the Lord's Prayer) until finally an unseen switch is activated, the plush curtains slide silently open and the coffin, bearing the mortal remains of the loved one, makes its dignified way into the cremation chamber.

The fact that the conversation among the guests, who line up to greet the relatives of the deceased in the covered walkway outside the chapel, may turn to such concerns as where to get a coffee, the whereabouts of the nearest tube station or the latest cricket scores, is comprehensible. Anything else is too near the knuckle. Friends and family murmur among themselves as the prayer hall fills up once more with mourners culled from a seemingly never-ending supply. Once again they are welcomed by the 'meeters and greeters' in their sober suits who have seen it all so very many times before.

Whether this dignified ceremony, culminating in cremation, is better or worse than the prayers and exhortations offered
at religious services held in churches, synagogues and mosques
– after which the bodies of the deceased are committed to
graves where tombstones will mark their resting places – is a
moot point. A more pressing one, for the next of kin as they
leave the crematorium, is how to dispose of the ashes. Or not.

While in the past the cremation option was embraced
mainly by the upper classes, as time goes by it has become
more popular, perhaps because disposing of a body in this efficient fashion is more direct. It is the ashes, and what to do with
them, that pose the problem, and more than 50 per cent are
left to line the shelves of the crematorium where, carefully
named and numbered, they are apt to languish.

The most popular 'scattering' places for the contents of the
green boxes or green urns with their screwtop lids, is a favourite venue of the loved one. What is not generally known is that
human ashes, far from fertilizing gardens and flower-beds – a
common fallacy – are highly toxic. They burn lawns and have a
particularly damaging effect upon roses (a popular choice) if
they do not actually kill them. Other favoured scattering places
are beauty spots, football pitches and sports arenas, mountains
and hilltops, beaches and bluebell woods, depending upon
the necessary permissions being granted, the local environment and the predilections of the deceased. The remains of
Hindus, Christians, atheists, sailors and boatmen are often
consigned to rivers, lakes and the sea, where, on a windswept
day, mortal remains have been known to blow back into the

faces of the scatterers and into their mouths. This hazard is not mentioned in a leaflet put out by the Environment Agency which states that 'the site you choose must *not* be near buildings, people bathing or marinas. On a river, ashes must be disposed of one kilometre upstream of any water abstraction, as close to the surface of the water as possible and not on windy days.' More bizarre outposts for internment in the USA – the Stratosphere Tower in Las Vegas, the Haunted House in Disneyland or the base of the Washington Memorial – present their own problems.

Ashes may also be buried in cemeteries, stored behind plaques in crematoria or portioned out, teaspoon by teaspoon, and left in meaningful places. Another novel if bizarre way of disposing of remains, which are sometimes sent to heaven in a firework, is to convert them into keepsakes, glass jewellery, charm beads and memorial rings for women mourners and silver pendants and glass-topped walking sticks for men.

With all these available options it is little wonder that, in many cases, the relatives of the departed end up paralysed by indecision and doing absolutely nothing at all. Whether it is distaste or inertia is by no means clear, but the urns and caskets, containing what is left of their nearest and dearest, are frequently delivered to the deceased's home where they ultimately become fixtures. All over Britain (*pace* a decree by the Vatican forbidding it for Roman Catholics) there are small domestic shrines, urns, boxes and caskets in living-room cabinets or on mantelpieces, often surrounded by pertinent keepsakes – photographs, ornaments, spectacles – or in cupboards, intimate, enclosed and private, where the ashes are prone to languish. The longer one postpones the decision to allot the nearest and dearest a final resting-place the harder it becomes to let his or her remains go: the truth of the matter is that the bereaved partner or relative either does not wish to or cannot. Incapable of bidding the final farewell, they grapple their loved ones to their sides, talk to them, divulge their innermost secrets and in return – if only in their imaginations – they are given not only companionship but guidance.

Whether it is due to indecision or to uncertainty, whether there are unresolved issues of grief and loss, whether or not those left behind are anticipating their own eventual demise, is immaterial. The knowledge that the deceased is still around on the shelf or in the cupboard, that he or she is present and available at all times, profligate with love and advice – incomprehensible as it may seem to those who have not been there – is solace enough.

32

SICKNESS AND HEALTH

The illness is speaking for me because
I have asked it to do so.

– Franz Kafka

Illness has been defined as 'a disease or period of sickness affecting the body or mind'. In the absence of symptoms there is no disease.

For the Greeks disease could be gratuitous or it could be deserved, as when it was visited on one for a personal fault, a collective transgression or a crime of one's ancestors. Disease as a punishment is widespread in literature from Cresseid's leprosy in *The Testament of Cresseid* to Madame de Merteuil's smallpox in *Les Liaisons Dangereuses*.

Nothing is more punitive than to give a disease a meaning – that meaning invariably being a moralistic one – or to suggest that nature is taking revenge on a godless world. Napoleon, Ulysses S. Grant and Hubert Humphrey considered their cancers to be a reaction to political defeat, while Keats, Chekhov and Emily Brontë regarded theirs as a verdict of failure. In the late sixteenth and seventeenth centuries it was considered that 'the happy man would not get the plague', and today some pill-popping health freaks seem to behave as if death is an inconvenience that can be avoided by spending sufficient time in the gym.

According to Susan Sontag, author of *Illness as Metaphor*, 'patients who were instructed that they have unwittingly caused their disease are also made to feel that they have deserved it'. In 1919 Hitler accused the Jews of producing a racial tuberculosis, while the Nazis compared European Jewry both to syphilis and to a cancer that must be excised. In *The Magic Mountain* Thomas Mann suggested that disease was 'a disguised manifestation of the power of love' and that 'all disease is only love transformed'.

Concepts such as 'disease', 'health', 'illness', 'sickness' and 'healing' can often prove hard to define. Part of the reason for this is that they embody value judgements and are so rooted in metaphor that it is sometimes hard to elucidate exactly what the words mean.

According to the medical definition, 'disease' is a pathological process, most often physical, such as in the case of a sore throat, or undetermined in origin, such as in cases of depression. It is a feeling or experience of 'unhealth' that is singular to the patient. While this 'unhealthy' feeling often accompanies disease, the disease itself may not be apparent (as in the early stages of cancer or diabetes). Sometimes illness exists where there is no apparent disease. This can be thwarting to the GP who, on examining the patient, finds nothing untoward and shunts the individual off to the nearest hospital for a fruitless round of investigations. Sickness is a social role, a status, a negotiated position in which a bargain is struck between the person who is 'sick' and society which is prepared to recognize and sustain him. Sickness based on illness alone is an uncertain commodity, but even the possession of disease does not guarantee equity in sickness. Those with a 'chronic' disease are much less secure than those with an 'acute' one; those with a psychiatric anomaly less secure than those with a surgical one. Best is an acute physical disease, in a hitherto healthy patient, which is quickly determined by recovery (or death).

Disease is a pathological process that deviates from a biological norm, while illness is the patient's experience of poor health, sometimes when no disease can be found. A minority of those who consult their GPs for repeat prescriptions are simply seeking to establish a therapeutic relationship with someone who is willing and able to listen and to help. A 'patient' – someone who actively consults a doctor rather than just being on the books – does not necessarily refer to a person who actually has a disease, who feels ill or is recognized to be sick. The patient may want to talk to someone about himself or herself or simply to get an annual flu jab. Most of the time, however, he can be classified as having a disease, feeling ill or being recognized as sick.

With the advent of Smart health care and a new NHS health app, patients will be able to book or cancel appointments, check their symptoms and consult a 'virtual nurse' who will question them about their symptoms, book a doctor's appointment, give information about over-the-counter remedies or advise them to call 999. Unqualified call handlers on the 111 helpline will be replaced by automated 'chatbots', and the majority of interaction with the NHS will be on mobile phones or tablets. It is unclear how the app will be regulated, but 'stringent safeguards' have been promised on the dissemination of data.

We have come a long way since the 'old-fashioned' GP who knew his patients and their families from birth – and who had most likely delivered them – wandered into the kitchen on his house-calls to see what was cooking (hoping to be offered a taste) and not only examined the patient but took time to sort out the family dynamics which, in certain cases, might be responsible for the patient's 'illness'.

This comprehensive approach, in stark contrast to today's over-investigation of a single presenting symptom, was more what Hippocrates, in the late fifth century BC, had in mind when he formulated his oath – no longer taken by physicians – which stated, 'About whatever I may see or hear in treatment, or even without treatment, in the life of human beings, I will remain silent, holding such things to be unutterable', as well as asserting that doctors should act in the best interests of the patients and when unjust circumstances arose – if a certain life-prolonging drug was not freely available, for instance – they should do their best to correct the situation in the interest of the patient.

The Bible, which maintains that 'only God has the power to heal completely and utterly', has much to say on the subject of ill health. 'The Lord sustains them on their sickbed and restores them from their bed of illness.' And 'A peaceful heart leads to a healthy body; jealousy is like cancer in the bones.' If only it were so simple!

While not so very long ago terminally ill patients were cared for in overcrowded hospital wards or at home, which was unsatisfactory for both patient and carer (if there was anyone to care), the advent of the hospice movement in 1967 changed for ever the way patients are treated when faced with life-limiting illnesses such as heart failure, chronic lung and kidney disease, stroke, neurological conditions – such as Parkinson's disease – and the end-stages of Alzheimer's (a present-day scourge) or similar conditions.

Long-term illness, particularly when one is housebound, can often be accompanied by a sense of isolation as one is divorced from one's work, social life and friends. When one is virtually immobilized as a result of illness the outlook can be pretty bleak. The rise of the hospice movement, which relies on voluntary support, donations from individuals, bequests in memory of loved ones and fund-raising events, has meant the provision of 'free' ongoing care and support for terminally ill patients at the most difficult and stressful time in their lives. As Bob Dylan put it, 'If You Gotta Go, Go Now'. The more than 3,000 hospices in the UK have not succeeded in moving life's mysterious goal-posts, but they have massively improved the end-game.

So much for illness. Today's obsession with health, in the guise of running, walking, cycling, trampolining, jogging, 'gym-ing' – going to the gym on a regular basis – not to mention dieting, which entails slavish dedication to ingesting or eschewing certain foods deemed to be 'good' or 'bad', can be regarded as a disease in itself.

According to the World Health Organization, health is not merely the absence of disease or infirmity but a state of complete physical, mental and social well-being in which one can express the full range of one's unique potential. Physical health is defined as something a person can achieve by developing all health-related components of his or her lifestyle. It reflects a person's cardio-respiratory endurance, muscular strength, flexibility and body composition. Other factors in well-being include proper nutrition – not just the latest fad – bodyweight management, avoiding drug and alcohol abuse and sexual health. Mental health refers to cognitive and emotional well-being which enables people to cope with stress and to work productively. It is easier to explain what mental 'illness' is, rather than to define mental 'health', the assessment of which is subjective but which include the ability to enjoy life, to cope with adversity, to feel safe and secure and to make the best of what you have.

'Wellness', the integration of mind, body and spirit, is, like the fashionable 'mindfulness' (a mental state apparently achieved by following one's awareness of the present moment while calmly acknowledging and accepting one's own feelings, thoughts and bodily sensations), is when we balance the physical, intellectual, emotional, social, occupational, spiritual and environmental aspects of life, in order to realize our goals and achieve our 'true potential'! It enables those of us lucky enough to have it to maintain an inner equilibrium (homeostasis). If you believe this gobbledegook you will be likely to latch on to any current 'health' mantra, slavish adherence to which is an 'illness' in itself.

We live in the age of the 'pop-up' health guru, many of whom are on power trips and purport to be authorities on how we should lead our lives. Tapping in to our insecurities, they take our money in exchange for information, knowledge or 'higher wisdom and advice' that is freely available to everyone. Frequently abusive, and threatening their adherents with what would happen to them if they *don't* buy into their beliefs, they charge extortionate fees for 'guidance' and laugh all the way to the bank. While many model themselves on the genuine article – the Indian sages who instruct their followers on how to live better and more fulfilled lives – others propagate spiritual nonsense that results in neither good health nor spiritual growth.

'Caveat emptor'; if you want to stay healthy, both physically and mentally, cultivate your friendships, expand your mind, listen to your body, eat a balanced diet, take exercise, get plenty of sleep and make a friend of your GP, even if he is inextricably attached to the umbilical cord of his computer.

33

GOING TO
THE DOCTOR

The good physician treats the disease; the great
physician treats the patient who has the disease.
– William Osler

While trying to cram our current ailments into the allotted ten
minutes, during which your general practitioner or GP barely
removes his eyes from the computer screen and seldom has time
to carry out a physical examination, it is hard to believe that in
the early days of the National Health Service the doctor with
whom you were registered single-handedly provided 24-hour
cover, carried out home visits, performed minor surgery, looked
after his patients in community hospitals and provided a host of
other services not directly remunerated.

In those pioneering days the GP was paid *per capita*. The
more patients he had on his 'list', the more money he received.
To lose a patient – or indeed an entire family – to a rival practitioner was a matter of financial concern. Competition was
intense, and to upset anyone by refusing to visit him or her, no
matter how trivial the complaint, was more than the doctor –
especially if he was the breadwinner of the family – could afford
to do. If a baby wouldn't stop crying, if an infant had a 'runny
nose' or a woman 'didn't like the look of her husband', off he had

to go. Driving in all weathers and at all times of day (or night), running up several flights of concrete stairs in high-rise apartment buildings – with a stethoscope and a packed bag of panaceas – to find a snivelling toddler playing happily with his toys or a patently hung-over adult sleeping it off in an armchair did nothing to improve the doctor–patient relationship which worsened even further with the eye-popping demands for 'free' prescriptions, many of which would end up being poured down the kitchen sink.

Requests for the 'white medicine' for indigestion or the 'brown bottle' for coughs were frequently couched in the form of vaguely concealed threats. By the same token, prescriptions for free bandages – destined for lampshade-making – or cotton-wool, which had been known to have been used to stuff soft toys, were extorted on pain of defection. Unlike in today's health centres where the practitioners, with their digitalized check-in screens and reception desks manned by 'patient-police' – who would threaten to have you blackballed rather than allow you to step out of line appointment-wise – it was the patients, sometimes as many as 3,000 of them, who, with one eye on a more obliging GP near by, had the upper hand.

While today it is no enviable task to be a 'family doctor', in the old days, the GP –whose Christmas sideboard groaned beneath the weight of 'bottles' from grateful patients – was king. Skilled in diagnoses, reached in part by his intimate knowledge of those on his 'list', many of whom over the years had become his friends, the doctor not only listened and observed but with little or no recourse to the diagnostic aids we now take for granted treated 'the whole person'. In the absence of technology, through which today he can access medical histories and drug regimes at the touch of a button, he called not only upon his medical knowledge but also his five senses to come to what was more often than not a pretty accurate diagnosis. With no CAT, ultrasound or MRI scans at his disposal and no ancillary help in his surgery (other than perhaps an obliging and overworked wife, the GP's being mostly male), armed with only the ubiquitous oversized syringe of penicillin, he may have taken more than ten minutes to reach a conclusion, but by using his hands, his eyes and his ears to make a diagnosis it was generally spot on. Taking his time, and getting to know the patient, were two weapons in his armoury, and his rigorous training had taught him to put them to good use.

How can the GP assess a harassed single mother presenting with nefarious pains and in need of social support, rather than medical care, in today's allotted ten minutes? If the patient in front of him has lost her appetite, has a pain in her back and a mysterious swelling on her big toe, which of her symptoms will he choose to explore? By the time she has removed her clothes (multi-layered in winter) and struggled on to the examination couch and he has employed his diagnostic skills (if he has not forgotten them) and entered his findings on the computer and waited while the woman dressed, more than ten minutes will have elapsed. The loss of time is exponential. The patients, many of whom have jobs or other commitments to honour, will be angry and the ancillary help, dedicated to make the practice run smoothly, frustrated. This unsatisfactory state of affairs may keep the practice ticking over, but it is exasperating for support staff, less than helpful for the patients and unsatisfactory for the GP. As he rushes through the day, chasing his own tail, it is almost impossible to employ 'best practice'. Terrified of overlooking some vital information, he is forever swimming against the tide of humanity who (eyes glued to the television in the reception area informing them how to get contraceptive advice, the consequences of drink-driving and the importance of regular flu jabs) wait, with embarrassment at the public exposure, for their names to come up on the screen.

This situation has been brought about by the deluge of NHS red tape which today makes so many demands upon the GP that corners must be cut. As the actual time the over-burdened doctors are able to spend with their patients dwindles, they find themselves adrift in a sea of bureaucracy as they share information with colleagues, fill in an avalanche of forms, forward requests to district nurses, physiotherapists and occupational therapists, write letters of referral to consultants and hospital departments, issue sick notes and repeat prescriptions – which must be carefully monitored – carry out the occasional home visit and, last but not least, attempt to have a life. It is little wonder that in a recent survey one in three GPs was considering retirement in the next five years, while nine out of ten reported that the workload was detrimental to their health.

While general practice was once a vocation, today – in addition to channelling patients through their ten-minute slots – the GP is expected to lead and manage a 'primary care team' and do much of what, in the old days, was done by specialists. Whereas the hospital out-patients clinics would once be full of patients attending for routine follow-ups, now they beleaguer the GP who, drowning in bureaucracy, spends precious hours documenting health outcomes and preparing for the inspections of the Care Quality Commission. He no longer has the time to be kind and to listen, to carry out school medicals, to run the family planning clinic or to be part of a community. While he is expected to manage 80 per cent of health problems for 8 per cent of the NHS budget, he is not only largely unappreciated by disgruntled patients – no bottle-strewn sideboard at Christmas – but must endure vilification of his profession by the media.

Despite the frustrating ten-minute consultation times, despite the unacceptable waiting-lists and inevitable hospital bed-blocking by the increasing number of elderly people who are unable to be discharged into the community, despite our health service's many faults, our GPs are hard-working, dedicated and clinically competent and our NHS, free at the point of delivery albeit funded by taxes, is the envy of the world. Computed tomography, magnetic resonance imaging and blood tests, however, are already abused and have the potential of leading to medical harm, while diagnostic uncertainty ignites extreme anxiety in patients. Corporate medicine and the drug industry, the new riders of the apocalypse, are making us all health neurotics, the result of which is the exponential growth of 'non-disease'.

As we follow advice from multifarious and dubious sources, take the pills, have unnecessary check-ups, monitor ourselves with 'health apps' and ground-breaking technology that will eventually link up with medical records and improve health care, we are deluded into the belief that by such means we will avoid getting such illnesses as cancer, dementia or heart disease.

It will not be long before 'virtual nurses' replace unqualified call-handlers, advise on over-the-counter remedies or urge patients to call 'help lines' manned by 'automated chatbots' who will monitor our vital signs via smartphones. Intended to empower patients, these devices, as yet untested, will open the door to greater anxiety and more neuroses.

While we already have a 'health-fixated' generation who are becoming more digitally savvy, and 'fitness' – in the guise of personal trainers, running the half-marathon and riding bikes that cost more than cars – has become the new obsession, who will interpret the results of these activities checked regularly on gadgets worn on the wrist and accessed on tablets and phones? Are these neurotic individuals aware how common 'brief' cardiac arrhythmias are or how frequently a blood-pressure reading is likely to be at a 'normal' high? Is humanity wasting its time on monitoring life rather than getting on with it? In the light of this robotic approach to health – 'if the system tells you you're fine you're probably fine' – the 'ten-minute' face-to-face slot with a GP, who has spent long years in medical school gathering data and passing stringent examinations and who has your medical history in front of him, must be the preferred option. General practice was, and still is, the backbone of the NHS. GPs, in their role as patients' advocates, gatekeepers and sorters of symptoms, keep our health service safe and accessible and provide value for money.

Today's GPs might be an endangered species, but what if they disappear?

34

PEACE AND WAR

Love is like war: easy to begin but very
hard to stop.

– H.L. Mencken

On Tuesday 8 May 1945, Victory in Europe Day, London was
one big party. It seemed as if the entire population had taken
to the streets. I was sixteen years old, and, sick with disgust and
for reasons entirely personal, I did not join in the jiving and
jitterbugging. The revellers, many of them drunk and disinhib-
ited, releasing joyful feelings which had been suppressed for
so long, seemed to me to be dancing on the graves of the thousands of young men who had lost their lives in the five-year
battle against 'brute force, bad faith, injustice, oppression and
persecution'.

The Second World War was the least unexpected war in history. My childhood coincided with a steady drift towards it as
sotto voce conversations, which I was not supposed to hear,
changed gradually from 'if' the war comes to 'when'.

By the middle of 1939 we had already become familiar with
'black-out' (to protect against the danger of air attack after night-
fall), the ululations of the air-raid siren – the sound of which still
evokes recollections of things past – and acronyms such as WVS
(Women's Voluntary Service) and ARP (Air Raid Precautions).

At school, jingoistic tunes such as 'Land of Hope and Glory' and 'I Vow to Thee My Country' had replaced traditional hymns, in an effort to sing away the conflict, and in the playground we skipped to

> Under the spreading chestnut tree,
> Neville Chamberlain said to me:
> 'If you want to get your gas mask free,
> Join the blinking ARP.'

Seen through a 78-year-old mirror, memories must of necessity be distorted. Be that as it may, mine, preserved in the formaldehyde of sadness both public and private, are still reflected with considerable clarity.

By any account, mine was not a 'bad' war. Compared with the sufferings of the millions in Europe, the fact that a teenage girl had to 'make do and mend', restrict herself to five inches of water in the bath (according to the Ministry of Fuel edict) and stand in line for several hours for three herrings was of little significance.

Despite minor inconveniences and deprivations, which after a while we came to accept as normal, I went neither cold nor hungry, but, suddenly burdened with responsibilities beyond my age, I progressed from childhood to adulthood without the indulgence of adolescence.

When at 11.15 a.m. on the crisp autumn morning of Sunday 3 September 1939 the Prime Minister, Mr Neville Chamberlain, made his announcement from the cabinet room of No. 10 Downing Street telling us that we were 'at war with Germany',

I was, on what was to be the last summer holiday for many years, with my parents and grandparents at a south coast English seaside resort.

The guests were gathered round the wireless set on the hotel reception desk when Mr Chamberlain's announcement was made. As they joined, self-consciously, in the National Anthem which followed the broadcast and tried to reassure one another that 'it would all be over by Christmas' I looked at the tears sliding surreptitiously down some of their faces and could not understand why they were crying.

Many of them were, of course, still licking their wounds from the 1914–18 débâcle, during the course of which some twelve million lives were arbitrarily snuffed out. They were remembering, with some bitterness, the 'war to end all wars' and anticipating with the knowledge of hindsight – especially those with sons or grandsons eligible for National Service – the dark days which they, but not I, knew lay ahead.

While many children, some as young as four and five, were separated from their parents and, with labels round their necks, boarded trains for foster homes in rural areas (evacuation was voluntary but billeting compulsory), I was lucky enough to be evacuated, together with my family, to the country, although I had only a vague idea of why this cataclysmic upheaval was taking place. Today's streetwise ten- and-eleven-year-olds may find this ignorance hard to understand, but mine was a generation in which many middle-class children were not only expected to be seen but not heard but were paternalistically protected from what was taking place in the world around them, which was considered strictly 'adult' business.

Our extended family was joined by a bewildered, intensely shy refugee boy with not a word of English, who came to England on the last *Kindertransport*. We had no idea what he was a refugee from and, consistent with past attitudes, we were never told. In the manner of children we accepted that he had left his family behind in Germany, but words such as *Kristallnacht*, Dachau, Theresienstadt and Belsen were yet to become part of the vernacular in Britain. My older brother, my younger sister and I had no notion of the Nazi persecution from which Max, our house-guest, had escaped, no idea how this bereaved child must be feeling, no inkling of the fact that he was never to see a single member of his large and loving family again.

I took the presence of Max (who quickly learned English) in our burgeoning household in my stride, in much the same way as I learned to put up the 'black-out' nightly on our many windows, preserve eggs laid by the chickens in our garden in buckets of water-glass (from which they often emerged stinking), make 'apricot flans' out of carrots and to 'dig for victory' – we grew all our own vegetables.

In a lull in the bombing we returned to London to be near my father – who was in the Royal Air Force (Special Investigation Branch) – in time for the 'Little Blitz'. At fifteen it was the most liberated and exciting time of my life, not least because the grown-ups were too busy helping the war effort to take much notice of what we did. We had to fend for ourselves. My memories of wartime London, illuminated by the glare of the searchlights which criss-crossed the night skies looking for enemy aircraft, are still lucid. Despite the poignant morning newspaper reports of digging for bodies in blocks of flats and streets of houses that had received direct hits – the flames more reminiscent of Dante's *Inferno* than the City of London which they consumed – there was no fear and little terror. As we waited with bated breath for the 'buzz bombs' or 'doodle bugs' (as the unmanned aircraft or 'V1's were known) to fall on someone else's house, and grew crick-necked from identifying enemy aircraft as 'theirs', it seemed more to be an exhilarating game of chance.

On one memorable day I came home from school, where lessons went on in the Anderson shelters as if it was the most natural thing in the world, to find that our flat had been devastated by the blast from a bomb – fortunately while we were all out – and we were homeless. The war was getting nearer. Later it was to brush my sleeve.

Unable to get any compensation for our lost home, we moved into a small family-run hotel where we were to live until the final all-clear. The son of the hotel proprietor, a handsome boy of nineteen, was in the Royal Air Force's Film Production Unit and flew on nightly sorties in Wellington bombers over Germany. It seemed inevitable that we not only fell in teenage love but that the war, which until now had seemed earnest only in the hearts of other people, took on a new dimension.

War not only intensifies passion but makes of time an infinitely precious commodity. Young people clung to each other unsure when or if they would meet again. The desperation of their kisses reflected the odds-on chance that each embrace was to be their last. If the songs were emotional ('I'll See You Again', 'Moonlight Becomes You' and 'Who's Taking You Home Tonight') and the dances sentimental, it was hardly surprising. The war had gone on too long. There was scarcely a family who had not lost life, limbs or a loved one. The lights had gone out all over Europe, and all at once it seemed – even to me – that Armageddon was fast approaching.

Wearing my pilot officer's 'wings' – in the shape of a gold brooch – and an RAF scarf in blue and maroon, I lived my life vicariously. I endured my boyfriend's mysterious and pro- longed absences, listened, terrified, to morning broadcasts – 'two of our aircraft were shot down' –and welcomed him back, exhausted and old beyond his years, in his flying boots and sheepskin jacket when he returned with matter-of-fact accounts of being hit by flak and 'near misses'. No thought was spared for the German crew of the Dorniers or Messerschmitts, boys as young as ours. It was kill or be killed, the law of the jungle.

I was so proud; to be seen with such a handsome young officer in Air Force uniform. The impenetrable streets and dark cinemas, with their long programmes – where they showed films such as *One Hundred Men and a Girl* and *The Stars Looked Down* – were hotbeds of romance. The words 'after the war' began to creep into our vocabulary and we made starry-eyed plans for the future.

In December 1944, when the conflict seemed to have only a few more months to run, my pilot officer was posted abroad to camps in France and Belgium. I began to receive letters, one almost every day 'On Active Service', postmarked 'Field Post Office', each one opened and read by the censor and marked with his stamp.

Unable to reveal what he was doing, the letters spoke only of 'hard work', mysterious 'jobs' which were 'on', 'bags of panic' and 'being very busy'. The mood of the unit was one of intense boredom, longing to come home, dislike of the desperate cold, lack of baths and of frozen pipes. Only when the air crews saw at first hand what the Belgian families in the villages where they were billeted had suffered during the German occupation did they realize exactly what it was for which they were fighting.

My pilot officer's next leave was due in April 1945. His letters were full of relief at the fact that at last the war seemed to be winding down, coupled with reassurances of love and plans for his homecoming.

On 30 March 1945, five weeks before the war in Europe officially ended, a telegram from the Air Ministry was delivered to the owner of the private hotel. 'Regret to inform you that your son —— is reported missing and believed to have lost his life as the result of air operations on 21 of March. Any further information will be communicated to you immediately.'

The stark telegram from the Air Ministry, facsimiles of which had been delivered daily to households up and down the land, brought home to me the fact that the past five years represented more than civilian hardship and deprivation, more than a matter of collecting wastepaper and scrap iron and standing in line for food. It was my first intimation of the real implications of conflict.

After the horror of this personal loss, which has stayed with me to this day, came the greater horror of the general one, as the newspapers, beneath pictures of scenes never before witnessed, began to play the numbers game, rough-guessing the total of lives lost in the concentration camps. These were my brethren. There, but for the grace of God and the fact that my grandparents had many years ago fled Poland and Holland respectively and settled in England, went I.

For these reasons I could not bring myself to watch the fancy-dress parties on Victory in Europe Day in 1945, to witness the carnival which, although there was much to celebrate, trod on far too many toes.

Had the boy aircrews of those Dorniers and Messerschmitts lived to tell the tale, their great-grandsons and great-granddaughters might well have been backpacking today in Manchester and Munich. The youth hostels of Europe are redolent with their ghosts, as new generations wander freely across the *schengen* borders and reap the freedom sown with the sacrificial blood of their forefathers.

35

THE NEXT BIG THING

When I have fears that I may cease to be
Before my pen has glean'd my teeming brain . . .
– John Keats

'One should attempt to write as if posthumously' was the late columnist Christopher Hitchens's take on mortality, while in the opposite camp Woody Alan quips nervously, 'I'm not afraid of dying. I just don't want to be there when it happens.'

Unfortunately we all live under the sentence of death, and we all are going to be there when it happens. While many of us, especially when we are young and the juices are flowing, give little thought to the 'final curtain', those who have been fortunate enough to reach old age have a different take on the matter. As we watch our friends and acquaintances tumble from their perches, and we get to attend more funerals than weddings, thought must inevitably be given to a life event which even the wiliest of us cannot avoid. Why must our time on earth – when we were doing very nicely, thank you – be curtailed so inescapably just as we were getting ready for it?

George Bernard Shaw had the right idea, and his pithy words on the subject are an inspiration for the writer whose *chef d'oeuvre* is always going to be the *next* book or play. 'I want to be thoroughly used up when I die, for the harder I work, the more I live.

I rejoice in life for its own sake. Life is no "brief candle" to me. It is a sort of splendid torch which I have got hold of for the moment; and I want to make it burn as brightly as possible before handing it on to future generations.' A lofty declaration and a position all of us would take if we could.

What is it we fear? Missing out on something? That we will be forgotten? Of course we will be forgotten, although those of us who have left some imprint on the sands of time hope that the written word will prevail and in the digital future, when the book, as we once knew it, has finally given way to technology, we may yet be 'discovered' – by those who have learned the dead language – on the dusty shelves of sec-ond-hand booksellers who still trade in that oddity the printed word.

According to Freud, people who express death-related fears are trying to deal with unresolved childhood conflicts with which they have not yet come to terms. Unless we are in psycho-analysis this is not much help. Childhood was a very long time ago and has receded into the distance together with youth and middle age. Death, which has, in the words of John Webster, 'ten thousand several doors for men to take their exits', is the next big thing. While men might seek to stop the clock by imitating the biblical King David and sleeping between two virgins, and women to cheat the grim reaper by opting for injections of monkey glands or indulging in a spot of gene therapy, no one has yet succeeded in delaying the inevitable or in borrowing any time worth mentioning.

Far from being irreplaceable, it is right and proper that we should be replaced. Fantasies of staying the hand of mortality are incompatible with the best interests not only of our species but of our children from whose memories, with the best will in the world, we will sooner or later fade. No matter how important your place in their lives, no matter how wonderful a mother, father, grandmother, grandfather you were, there will come a time when your family will think of you less often, will accept your absence and proceed with business as usual. That there are clearly defined limits to our lives must be accepted, and death comes more easily to those who have given it the most thought. It might help to remember that nobody goes out struggling.

You will die. And not only will you die, but everyone you love and who loves you will die, and, one day, whether it is in 100 or 100,000 years hence, there will be no memory, trace or evidence that you once lived. What are you to do about it other than live in the moment with as much passion and strength as you can summon. Life is not a dress rehearsal, and time is running out.

As the adolescent sees in the middle aged the ageing that comes with the second half of life, so those who are middle aged see in the generation above them an inescapable physical decline and subsequent loss of independence. While some of these elderly people will feel worthless and unwanted, those lucky enough to be both healthy and creative will march to 'inner' rather than 'outer' time', which helps to keep uncomfortable thoughts and feelings at bay. Michael Tippett and Georges Solti in the world of music, Pablo Picasso in the world of visual art and many writers in their seventies and eighties have demonstrated in their later works that age and experience enhance their creativity and that, in the words of Jung, 'The afternoon of life is just as full of meaning as the morning; only its meaning and purpose are different.'

As far as I am concerned, the spectacle of insanity and senility scares me more than does the witnessing or the hearing of a physical death. This premature death of the human spirit can be more distressing than the deterioration of the body. The 'light of reason' makes us human, and when our outer world begins to diminish, feelings of isolation and inner loneliness ensue, largely through the inevitable loss of lifelong friends. As Margaret Mead put it, 'Having someone wonder where you are when you don't come home at night is a very human need.'

It is reassuring to know that one matters to another human being, that one is not alone. Sadly this is not always the case, which is borne out by the proliferation of 'care' and 'nursing' homes in which abandoned relatives, many of whom have once lived happy and productive lives, sit round the walls observing the inevitability of death and contemplating their own.

As we project our own fears of growing old and of death on to the older generation – who are not only who they appear to be but an amalgam of the many selves they have been before – we see them as a threat to our own lifestyles and are fearful of the demands they might make on us. We are distressed at the inevitable change we perceive in ageing relatives – many of whom may feel worthless, unwanted and depressed – not least because they remind us of what is in store for us. Lumping them together, if we notice them at all, is to isolate them from the human race. While the young search for freedom from being dependent and long for independence, those in the second half of life look for someone on whom they can reliably depend and to whom they can feel close. In many cases this search is fruitless and loneliness is compounded. As Montaigne expressed it, 'The utility of living consists not in the length of days but in the use of time; a man may have lived long yet lived but a little.'

The great bogeyman of today, feared almost more than death itself, is one Alois Alzheimer, a twentieth-century clinician interested in nervous and mental diseases and, in particular, in pre-senile dementia. What is widely known as 'Alzheimer's' disease' – in which there are successive symptoms of jealousy, loss of memory and reasoning powers, paranoia and incomprehension – is a distressing condition which strikes indiscriminately. While the symptoms are irreversible, strip the patient of dignity and may persist for many years, the suffering may be mitigated by the support and closeness of such friends and family whose love and loyalty transcends the mental and physical decline of their loved one.

Growing well into old age is not about striving to be young. It involves acknowledging oneself and one's life, in all its complexities, as it once was and as it is now. It is about accepting both the positive and negative sides of others, about putting up with loss and disability as well as embracing opportunities for new experiences. Most important of all, it is about developing a balance of hope over despair

AFTERWORD

Old men must die, or the world would grow
mouldy, would only breed the past again.
– Alfred, Lord Tennyson

Whatever one does in one's life is one's own responsibility and cannot be changed. How scary is that? And possibly the scariest part is that this realization doesn't hit home until you're nearing the end of it. How can you be so sure? *Anno domini*; the ever increasing roll- call of deceased family, friends, colleagues and acquaintances, confirmed by the gaps – like missing teeth – in one's address book; the obituaries in the newspapers (more about the richness of life rather than about death) which one now scans eagerly to discover which of one's acquaintances, which famous figure who has helped shape the course of history, has moved on, leaving his or her imprint upon the sands of time.

Life hangs on a thread. Sometimes it is almost snuffed out before it begins, as was this unborn child's, when one eighteenth-century doctor said to another, 'I want your opinion about a possible abortion. The father is syphilitic, the mother has tuberculosis, the first child was born blind, the second died, the third could neither hear nor speak, and the fourth was tuberculous. What would you do?'

'I would terminate the pregnancy,' his colleague replied.

'Then you would have murdered Beethoven?'

Transience is brought home when, one by one, friends and relatives begin to 'shuffle off their mortal coils'. A heart attack here, a cancer ('battled against' or 'bravely borne') there; Alzheimer's, dementia, motor-neurone and Parkinson's diseases, organs that have failed; pancreases and kidneys, livers and lungs that have given up the ghost.

The time comes – often in one's ninth decade in these days of longevity – when, having travelled so far along the precipitous road of life, Mortality is no longer the perquisite of other, older or more vulnerable people but is doffing his hat on your doorstep.

The moment you realize that there is no escape, that one way or another, sooner or later, you will have to let him in; the moment one takes on board one's own vulnerability and the hand's-breadth of days that remain is the moment you determine to work harder than ever to leave your imprint upon the sands of time.

Here, of course, the writer, conscious like Andrew Marvell of 'Time's winged chariot hurrying near', has the advantage. While the bricklayer cannot go on laying bricks, nor the dentist continue to pull teeth, there is no reason for the artist or the author, provided that he or she is still *compos mentis*, to abandon the craft in which that individual has managed to navigate the choppy waters throughout his or her working life. It is the act of creation – the origins of which no one has as yet managed to explain – which takes you to another level in which the minutiae of daily life miraculously disappear and all pain and tribulation recede. If you are asked to explain it, you can't. This paradise, this illusion, this fantasy world you have been privileged to enter is a gift which has been bestowed upon you and the secret of which cannot be divulged. You cannot unlock it. If creation doesn't come, unbidden, directly from the unconscious mind and alight somewhere, by whatever agent you employ, in tangible form, it is a dull and worthless parody and not worth the paper (or computer) it is written on. While the composer is rarely asked to disclose the formula by which he comes up with a symphony or arrives at a sonata, the writer's secrets appear, to the outsider, to be rich pickings. The truth is that one doesn't know oneself what it is that spurs one on to create stories, and characters with which to inhabit those stories, to produce plays and poems, fiction and fantasy. It is what one has always done and which one will go on doing as long as one's strength and eyesight permits. Creation is the analgesic par excellence. The drawback is that as one grows older, while invention and fabrication do not necessarily dry up, the brain tires, the memory fades, the hands grow stiff, the back aches, the eyes grow dim and with these manifestations of age comes the realization that the clock is ticking.

This did not worry Montaigne. 'If you don't know how to die, don't worry. Nature will tell you what to do on the spot, fully and adequately. She will do this job perfectly for you; don't bother your head about it.'

As one by one friends and family shuffle off their mortal coils, it is the funerals, frequent and inevitable now, that remind us of our rightful place and become the *sine qua non* of our days. Be they accompanied by religious or atheist, traditional or humanist services and rituals, by burial or cremation, paradoxically they provide the writer with rich pickings.

As family, friends, colleagues and acquaintances are consigned to mud-clogged graves or in their recyclable coffins slide silently and seamlessly into burning pits, one is forced to confront one's own mortality and to wonder whether the struggling and striving, the triumphs and disappointments, the trials and tribulations that are the components of life have been worth it. While eulogies are delivered and the remains of loved ones are stashed in drawers or wardrobes to gather dust, while once familiar bodies are consigned to the clogged earth, we wonder – during this brief respite from our daily lives – when our turn will come and what it has all been for. We know about 'ashes to ashes' and 'dust to dust' and 'we shall not grow old as you who are left grow old'. But what does it all mean? No sooner have we turned our backs on the freshly dug sods or left the burial hall than the memories of our loved ones ebb, and life, in all its manifestations, goes on. As for making sense of it, should we even try?

Most religions have strong views regarding life and death. They range from belief in reincarnation, heaven and hell, to the equivocal 'ongoing of the soul' and the possibility of an afterlife which varies between denominations and individuals. Clinging to the biblical certitude that 'there is a time to be born and a time to die', Christians, who put their faith in Jesus, will achieve salvation and end up in heaven, while those who do not are destined for hell.

If you are a Muslim you will believe that the present life is but a preparation for the next realm of being. Death is the transition from one world to another, a journey through a separate dimension of existence. The Prophet teaches that three things can help a person, even after death: the charity which he has given, the knowledge which he has taught and the prayers said on his behalf by a righteous child. Upon death the body is washed and covered with a clean white cloth and laid on its right side facing the direction of Makkah or Mecca. Prayers are said, and preparations for the burial – as is also the Jewish custom – take place as speedily as possible.

In Hinduism there is a strong belief in the rebirth and reincarnation of the soul as a separate entity. When a person dies, the soul travels for some time to another world and finally returns to an afterlife on earth to continue its journey. Hindus are not buried but cremated. By burning the corpse – with its intrinsic rituals – the elements are rightly returned to their respective spheres, while the body, along with the soul, returns to the world for the continuation of the afterlife.

Much has been said about the significance of death in Buddhism. It was the awareness of death that prompted the Lord Buddha to explore the truth behind worldly concerns and pleasures and come to the conclusion that death is taking a break from the materialistic world and is not a continuation of the soul but an awakening. Once a person dies he or she will be reborn to a new life on earth, and the status of that life depends on the work that individual did while he was here. When someone is near to death, family members and monks recite scriptures and mantras in order to help him or her achieve a peaceful state of mind.

Judaism teaches the value of life above all else. Taking a single life is like destroying an entire world, and saving a single life is like saving an entire world. Death – even when premature or through unfortunate circumstances – is not a tragedy but a natural process, and the importance of life is the way in which it is lived on earth.What happens afterwards is in God's hands. Mourning practices show respect for the dead and provide comfort for the living. Jewish graves are marked with tombstones (as are Christian ones) on which the custom is for mourners to leave small stones, rather than flowers, as a mark of their visit.

While most people, certainly as they get older, have a vested interest in death and its mysteries, nearly all of us are fascinated by the *Register* pages of the daily newspapers which illuminate the lives of those who, for better or worse, have left their mark. As we trawl though these compelling snapshots of heroes and villains, of the great and the good, we are amazed to learn not only of their achievements, which may well be in the public domain, but intriguing facts about their early lives and relationships that make us wish we had known them better. Who would have guessed that an illustrious individual destined to shape the course of history was once a long-haired marijuana-fuelled hippie, or that some pillar of the establishment was not only rusticated from Oxbridge but spent his early years flogging dusters and brushes on suburban doorsteps.

The work of the obituarist is often full of surprises as he employs the conventions of his newspaper to indicate how one deceased favoured an 'open marriage' (that is, was promiscuous), while another 'never married' (that is, was gay), and their columns are not so much about the finality of 'death' but about the richness of lives, which sometimes turn out to be revelatory.

All you can hope for is that when your train arrives at its final destination the journey will have been painless and those you have loved will be waiting for you at the other end. What really draws us 'senior citizens' to the back pages, before we have even acquainted ourselves with the daily news – has yet to be determined. Rather than striving to uncover the secret, however, we should perhaps determine to 'live life to the full' before we end up between the 'Business' and the 'Weather'.